Try The Best Cholesterol Recipes: A Delicious New Cookbook

Easy, Quick, and Healthy Original Dishes with Vibrant Photos and Fresh Ideas

By Divvey Wazsoya

Copyright © [2023] Divvey Wazsoya

All rights reserved. This book or any portion thereof may not be reproduced or used in any manner whatsoever without the publisher's express written permission, except for the use of brief quotations in a book review or scholarly journal.

No part of this publication may be reproduced, distributed, or transmitted in any form or by any means, including photocopying, recording, or other electronic or mechanical methods, without the prior written permission of the publisher, except in the case of brief quotations embodied in critical reviews and specific other noncommercial uses permitted by copyright law.

All recipes, images, and content herein are the intellectual property of Divvey Wazsoya and may not be duplicated, redistributed, or repurposed without explicit permission.

All images in this book are copyright-protected and may not be used or reproduced without explicit permission from the copyright holder.

This publication is designed to provide accurate and authoritative information about the subject matter covered. While all efforts have been made to ensure the accuracy and completeness of the information contained in this book, the author and the publisher accept no responsibility for errors or omissions.

This book is intended for informational purposes only. The reader is encouraged to seek professional advice when required. Neither the author nor the publisher can be held liable for any losses, injuries, or damages resulting from applying the information in this book.

Introduction

Welcome to a culinary adventure tailored for the heart-smart and health-conscious! Have you ever felt the need to enjoy delectable dishes without the guilt of high cholesterol?

Dive into **"Try the Best 100 Low Cholesterol Recipes"** and discover a treasury of recipes that not only tantalize your taste buds but also promote a healthier lifestyle. Written with passion and precision by Divvey Wazsoya, each dish has been crafted considering flavor and well-being. Say goodbye to bland meals and hello to a world where low cholesterol doesn't compromise taste!

Imagine savoring mouth-watering daily meals, from creamy soups and crunchy salads to sumptuous entrees and delightful desserts, all while stepping towards a healthier heart. Each recipe comes alive with vibrant photos, making it an irresistible treat for the eyes even before you get cooking. With easy-to-follow steps and fresh ideas, this cookbook is both for the novice trying to cook for the first time and the seasoned chef looking for innovative low-cholesterol dishes.

So, why wait? Flip the pages and embark on a journey where each recipe promises a fusion of flavor and health. Whether you're cooking for one or a feast for many, this cookbook ensures every dish is a step towards a healthier you. Embrace a delicious way of living with **"Try the Best 100 Low Cholesterol Recipes" by Divvey Wazsoya**. Your heart (and taste buds) will thank you!

Table of Contents

Chapter 01: Heart-Healthy Morning 8
- Recipe 01: Sunrise Oatmeal with Fresh Berries 8
- Recipe 02: Fluffy Whole Wheat Pancakes 10
- Recipe 03: Morning Glory Smoothie Bowl 12
- Recipe 04: Almond Butter & Banana Toast 14
- Recipe 05: Heart-Healthy Avocado & Spinach Omelette 16
- Recipe 06: Nutty Granola Parfait 18
- Recipe 07: Chia Seed & Berry Pudding 20
- Recipe 08: Fresh Fig and Quinoa Breakfast Bowl 22
- Recipe 09: Omega-3 Packed Flaxseed Muffins 24
- Recipe 10: Spinach and Feta Breakfast Casserole 26

Chapter 02: Wholesome Brunch 28
- Recipe 11: Tropical Mango & Kiwi Salad 28
- Recipe 12: Quinoa & Almond Brunch Muffins 30
- Recipe 13: Heart-Smart Veggie Frittata 32
- Recipe 14: Avocado Toast with Pomegranate Seeds 34
- Recipe 15: Berry-Packed Chia Pudding 36
- Recipe 16: Spinach & Mushroom Mini Quiches 38
- Recipe 17: Sweet Potato & Kale Hash 40
- Recipe 18: Blueberry & Walnut Overnight Oats 42
- Recipe 19: Golden Turmeric Smoothie 44
- Recipe 20: Protein-Packed Chickpea Pancakes 46

Chapter 03: Lunches for Lively Hearts 48
- Recipe 21: Mediterranean Chickpea Salad 48
- Recipe 22: Grilled Chicken & Vegetable Wraps 50
- Recipe 23: Heart-Healthy Tuna Nicoise 52
- Recipe 24: Zesty Lentil & Spinach Soup 54
- Recipe 25: Whole Wheat Veggie Pizza 56

- Recipe 26: Roasted Veggie & Hummus Pita Pockets 58
- Recipe 27: Quinoa and Black Bean Bowl 60
- Recipe 28: Tomato & Basil Zoodles 62
- Recipe 29: Spiced Sweet Potato & Lentil Salad 64
- Recipe 30: Tofu & Vegetable Stir-Fry 66

Chapter 04: Guilt-Free Afternoon Nibbles 68

- Recipe 31: Nut & Seed Trail Mix 68
- Recipe 32: Kale & Sea Salt Chips 70
- Recipe 33: Fresh Veggie Sticks with Guacamole 72
- Recipe 34: Almond Joy Energy Bites 74
- Recipe 35: Garlic & Herb Popcorn 76
- Recipe 36: Cholesterol-Free Chocolate Mousse 78
- Recipe 37: Spiced Roasted Chickpeas 80
- Recipe 38: Olive & Tomato Bruschetta 82
- Recipe 39: Raspberry Almond Bliss Balls 84
- Recipe 40: Oven-Baked Sweet Potato Fries 86

Chapter 05: Delicious Dinners Low in Cholesterol 88

- Recipe 41: Lemon Herb Grilled Salmon 88
- Recipe 42: Whole Wheat Spaghetti with Fresh Tomato Sauce 90
- Recipe 43: Garlic-infused Olive Oil & Veggie Stir-Fry 92
- Recipe 44: Oven-Roasted Herb Chicken 94
- Recipe 45: Stuffed Bell Peppers with Quinoa & Veggies 96
- Recipe 46: Grilled Eggplant & Zucchini Platter 98
- Recipe 47: Vegan Thai Green Curry 100
- Recipe 48: Heart-Friendly Ratatouille 102
- Recipe 49: Barley & Vegetable Risotto 104
- Recipe 50: Lentil & Mushroom Stuffed Acorn Squash 106

Chapter 06: Light and Luscious 108

- Recipe 51: Dark Chocolate Covered Almonds 108

Recipe 52: Greek Yogurt & Mixed Berry Parfait 110

Recipe 53: Peanut Butter & Celery Sticks 112

Recipe 54: Cinnamon Spiced Apple Slices 114

Recipe 55: Light Popcorn with Nutritional Yeast 116

Recipe 56: Chilled Melon Balls 118

Recipe 57: Nutty Cocoa Energy Bites 120

Recipe 58: Banana & Almond Smoothie 122

Recipe 59: Rice Cakes with Avocado Spread 124

Recipe 60: Mixed Nuts with Dried Fruits...126

Chapter 07: Soul-Warming Soups with a Healthy Twist 128

Recipe 61: Hearty Lentil & Vegetable Soup 128

Recipe 62: Tomato Basil Bliss Soup 130

Recipe 63: Creamy Butternut Squash & Carrot Soup 132

Recipe 64: Clear Broth with Greens & Tofu 134

Recipe 65: Spinach & White Bean Soup 136

Recipe 66: Chilled Cucumber & Dill Soup 138

Recipe 67: Spicy Pumpkin & Ginger Soup 140

Recipe 68: Red Beet Borscht 142

Recipe 69: Heartwarming Mushroom & Barley Soup 144

Recipe 70: Refreshing Gazpacho 146

Chapter 08: Appetizers to Begin with a Beat 148

Recipe 71: Cherry Tomato & Basil Skewers 148

Recipe 72: Zucchini Rolls with Hummus & Peppers...................................150

Recipe 73: Mini Spinach & Feta Tarts..152

Recipe 74: Guacamole & Salsa Dip Duo 154

Recipe 75: Light Mozzarella & Olive Tapenade 156

Recipe 76: Stuffed Grape Leaves with Rice & Herbs 158

Recipe 77: Roasted Pepper & Walnut Spread 160

Recipe 78: Tofu Satay with Peanut Sauce..162

Recipe 79: Beetroot & Goat Cheese Crostini..164

Recipe 80: Chilled Avocado & Cilantro Soup Shots.....................................166

Chapter 09: Crunchy, Fresh Salads for a Strong Heart....................................168

Recipe 81: Green Goddess Kale & Avocado Salad 168

Recipe 82: Roasted Beet & Arugula with Walnuts..170

Recipe 83: Lively Lemon Quinoa Salad 172

Recipe 84: Summer Corn & Tomato Salad 174

Recipe 85: Heart-Healthy Greek Salad 176

Recipe 86: Rainbow Carrot & Radish Slaw 178

Recipe 87: Spinach, Orange, & Almond Delight 180

Recipe 88: Crispy Tofu & Broccoli Salad 182

Recipe 89: Mediterranean Bulgar & Chickpea Salad....................................184

Recipe 90: Fresh Herb & Mixed Greens Salad..186

Chapter 10: Party Plates: Celebrate the Low-Cholesterol Way 188

Recipe 91: Mini Veggie & Hummus Cups 188

Recipe 92: Olive Tapenade & Whole Wheat Crackers..................................190

Recipe 93: Baked Spinach & Artichoke Dip..192

Recipe 94: Heart-Friendly Mini Pizzas..194

Recipe 95: Grilled Asparagus with Lemon Zest..196

Recipe 96: Mixed Berry & Chia Seed Pudding Cups....................................198

Recipe 97: Pesto & Sun-Dried Tomato Pinwheels 200

Recipe 98: Seared Tuna Bites with Wasabi Dip 202

Recipe 99: Lemon & Herb Stuffed Mushrooms...204

Recipe 100: Dark Chocolate Dipped Strawberries 206

Conclusion 208

Chapter 01: Heart-Healthy Morning

Recipe 01: Sunrise Oatmeal with Fresh Berries

Navigating through the realm of heart-healthy recipes can sometimes feel like traversing a tasteless terrain. Yet, mornings are about to become radiant with the Sunrise Oatmeal with Fresh Berries, a dish that combines oats' wholesomeness with fresh berries' vibrancy. This simple recipe makes mornings delightful and ensures you begin your day with delicious nutrition.

Servings: 2

Prepping Time: 5 minutes

Cook Time: 10 minutes

Difficulty: Easy

Ingredients:

- 1 cup rolled oats
- 2 cups almond milk or water

- ❖ A pinch of salt
- ❖ 1 tablespoon honey or maple syrup (optional)
- ❖ 1/2 cup mixed fresh berries (strawberries, blueberries, raspberries)
- ❖ A sprinkle of chia seeds or flaxseeds for added nutrition (optional)

Step-by-Step Preparation:

- ✓ In a saucepan, bring the almond milk or water to a boil.
- ✓ Add the rolled oats and a pinch of salt. Reduce heat to medium and simmer, stirring occasionally.
- ✓ Cook until the oats have absorbed the liquid and are creamy about 7-10 minutes.
- ✓ Pour the oatmeal into bowls and top with fresh berries.
- ✓ Drizzle with honey or maple syrup, and sprinkle with chia or flaxseeds.

Nutritional Facts: (Per serving)

- ❖ Calories: 210
- ❖ Protein: 6g
- ❖ Carbs: 38g
- ❖ Fat: 4g
- ❖ Fiber: 6g
- ❖ Sugars: 10g

As you savor each spoonful, relish the perfect meld of the creaminess of the oatmeal and the burst of freshness from the berries. It's more than just a breakfast dish; it promises a heart-healthy, flavor-filled morning. Whether you're setting off for a strenuous day or a relaxing one, the Sunrise Oatmeal ensures you're fueled up, heart-healthy, and ready to face whatever the day brings. Enjoy this delightful start to your day.

Recipe 02: Fluffy Whole Wheat Pancakes

Ditch the misconception that hearty and healthy can't sit together on the same breakfast plate. You are introducing the Fluffy Whole Wheat Pancakes – a delightful blend of wholesome goodness with the fluffy texture you love. These pancakes, rich in fiber and nutrients, ensure your heart is as content as your taste buds when you take that first bite.

Servings: 4

Prepping Time: 10 minutes

Cook Time: 15 minutes

Difficulty: Intermediate

Ingredients:

- 1 cup whole wheat flour
- 1 tablespoon sugar (optional)
- 1 teaspoon baking powder
- 1/2 teaspoon baking soda
- A pinch of salt

- 1 cup buttermilk
- 1 large egg
- 2 tablespoons unsalted butter, melted

Step-by-Step Preparation:

- ✓ Whisk together the flour, sugar, baking powder, baking soda, and salt in a large mixing bowl.
- ✓ In another bowl, combine buttermilk, egg, and melted butter.
- ✓ Pour the wet ingredients into the dry ingredients and gently mix until combined. Avoid over mixing.
- ✓ Preheat a skillet over medium heat and lightly grease it.
- ✓ Pour 1/4 cup batter for each pancake until bubbles form on the surface, then flip and cook until browned on the other side.

Nutritional Facts: (Per serving)

- Calories: 185
- Protein: 6g
- Carbs: 30g
- Fat: 5g
- Fiber: 4g
- Sugars: 4g

Embarking on a heart-healthy journey doesn't mean bidding farewell to your favorite dishes. These Fluffy Whole Wheat Pancakes offer a tantalizing treat without skimping on taste or health benefits. Whether topped with fresh fruit, a drizzle of maple syrup, or eaten plain, they are the perfect heart-friendly canvas for your morning culinary creativity. Dive fork-first into a breakfast that both your heart and palate will appreciate.

Recipe 03: Morning Glory Smoothie Bowl

Embarking on a day filled with tasks and challenges necessitates a wholesome beginning. And what better way than with the Morning Glory Smoothie Bowl, a symphony of vibrant flavors and nutritional powerhouses? Designed to invigorate your senses and infuse your body with much-needed nutrients, this breakfast option ensures you start your day on a heart-healthy note without compromising taste.

Servings: 2

Prepping Time: 10 minutes

Cook Time: 0 minutes

Difficulty: Easy

Ingredients:

- 1 ripe banana
- 1/2 cup frozen mixed berries
- 1/2 cup Greek yogurt
- 1/4 cup rolled oats

- 1 tablespoon chia seeds
- 1/2 cup almond milk
- Toppings: sliced fruits, nuts, seeds, or granola

Step-by-Step Preparation:

- ✓ Combine banana, frozen berries, Greek yogurt, rolled oats, chia seeds, and almond milk in a blender.
- ✓ Blend until smooth and creamy.
- ✓ Pour the mixture into bowls.
- ✓ Garnish with your choice of toppings.

Nutritional Facts: (Per serving)

- Calories: 210
- Protein: 8g
- Carbs: 36g
- Fat: 5g
- Fiber: 7g
- Sugars: 18g

The allure of the Morning Glory Smoothie Bowl goes beyond its vibrant appearance. It's a medley of heart-healthy ingredients designed to nourish you from the inside out. Every spoonful is packed with vitamins, minerals, and antioxidants, ensuring that your morning isn't just delightful and beneficial for your heart's well-being. Whether rushing to a meeting or enjoying a lazy Sunday morning, this smoothie bowl caters to your health and taste with equal enthusiasm. Relish it, and let your day bloom with this bowl's energy and vibrancy.

Recipe 04: Almond Butter & Banana Toast

Finding that perfect blend of simplicity, taste, and nutrition can sometimes feel like chasing a mirage. But with the Almond Butter and banana Toast, the search ends on a delightful note. Combining the natural sweetness of bananas with the creamy richness of almond butter, this toast offers a quick yet heart-healthy breakfast solution bound to kickstart your day with energy and flavor.

Servings: 2

Prepping Time: 5 minutes

Cook Time: 2 minutes

Difficulty: Easy

Ingredients:

- 2 slices of whole-grain bread
- 4 tablespoons almond butter
- 1 ripe banana, sliced
- A sprinkle of chia seeds (optional)

- ❖ A drizzle of honey (optional)

Step-by-Step Preparation:

- ✓ Toast the whole grain bread slices until they are golden and crispy.
- ✓ Generously spread almond butter on each slice.
- ✓ Arrange the banana slices over the almond butter.
- ✓ If desired, sprinkle with chia seeds and drizzle with honey.

Nutritional Facts: (Per serving)

- ❖ Calories: 295
- ❖ Protein: 8g
- ❖ Carbs: 35g
- ❖ Fat: 15g
- ❖ Fiber: 7g
- ❖ Sugars: 10g

The Almond Butter and banana Toast isn't just a breakfast dish; it's a declaration that heart-healthy meals can be uncomplicated and utterly delicious. Every bite is packed with nutrients that cater to your heart, fueling your morning with the right blend of carbs, proteins, and healthy fats. Perfect for those on-the-go mornings or when you want something straightforward yet fulfilling, this toast is the epitome of health meets taste. As you savor each mouthful, let the textures and flavors remind you of the simple joys of a wholesome breakfast. Embrace the morning with this toast by your side.

Recipe 05: Heart-Healthy Avocado & Spinach Omelette

Dive into a morning feast that contradicts the norm: introducing the "Heart-Healthy Avocado & Spinach Omelette" within a beef stir fry framework. This breakfast treat blends the rich, buttery texture of avocado with the wholesome goodness of spinach; all wrapped up in a succulent beef stir fry. It's a culinary union that champions' heart health without compromising flavor, making it the ideal dish to kick starts Heart-Healthy Morning.

Servings: 2

Prepping Time: 15 minutes

Cook Time: 20 minutes

Difficulty: Intermediate

Ingredients:

- 4 large eggs
- 1 ripe avocado, diced
- 1 cup fresh spinach, washed and chopped

- 200g lean beef, thinly sliced
- 2 tbsp olive oil
- Salt and pepper to taste
- 2 cloves garlic, minced
- 1 tbsp soy sauce (low sodium)
- 1 tsp ginger, grated

Step-by-Step Preparation:

- ✓ In a bowl, whisk the eggs, adding salt and pepper to taste. Set aside.
- ✓ In a skillet, heat 1 tbsp of olive oil over medium heat. Add garlic and ginger, sautéing briefly.
- ✓ Add thinly sliced beef to the skillet and stir fry until browned.
- ✓ Mix in soy sauce and continue stir-frying for another 2 minutes.
- ✓ Push beef to one side of the skillet and pour in the beaten eggs on the other.
- ✓ Scatter the spinach and diced avocado on top of the eggs.
- ✓ As the omelet is set, gently fold it over the beef stir fry.
- ✓ Cook until the eggs are fully set. Slide onto a plate and serve hot.

Nutritional Facts: (Per serving)

- Calories: 385
- Protein: 28g
- Fats: 25g
- Carbohydrates: 10g
- Fiber: 6g
- Sodium: 410mg
- Cholesterol: 380mg

Breakfasts that redefine the culinary landscape while emphasizing heart health are few and far between. The Heart-Healthy Avocado & Spinach Omelette with a beef stir fry twist is one such dish, perfectly balancing nutrition and taste. As the inaugural recipe of our "Heart-Healthy Morning" chapter, it showcases the delightful possibilities of combining traditional breakfast elements with lunchtime favorites. Celebrate your mornings with this heart-nourishing and palate-pleasing creation, setting a healthy and delicious tone for the day ahead.

Recipe 06: Nutty Granola Parfait

Venture into a surprising twist with the "Nutty Granola Parfait" in the mold of a beef stir fry recipe. Traditionally, granola parfaits are sweet, crunchy, and layered delights. This innovative recipe combines the heart-healthy grains of a classic parfait with the savory zest of beef stir fry, creating a fusion breakfast dish for our Heart-Healthy Morning.

Servings: 2

Prepping Time: 10 minutes

Cook Time: 15 minutes

Difficulty: Intermediate

Ingredients:

- 1 cup granola
- 1/2 cup Greek yogurt
- 200g lean beef, thinly sliced
- 2 tbsp soy sauce (low sodium)
- 1 tbsp honey

- 1 tsp ginger, grated
- 2 cloves garlic, minced
- 2 tbsp olive oil
- 1/4 cup mixed nuts (almonds, walnuts, pecans), chopped
- Fresh berries for garnish

Step-by-Step Preparation:

- In a skillet, heat olive oil over medium heat. Add garlic and ginger, sautéing briefly.
- Introduce the thinly sliced beef and stir fry until it's browned.
- Drizzle in the soy sauce and honey until the beef is well-coated.
- Layer a spoonful of granola in serving glasses or bowls at the base.
- Add a layer of the beef stir fry on top of the granola.
- Spoon a layer of Greek yogurt over the beef.
- Sprinkle the chopped mixed nuts.
- Repeat the layers until the glass is full, finishing with a yogurt layer.
- Garnish with fresh berries on top.

Nutritional Facts: (Per serving)

- Calories: 460
- Protein: 32g
- Fats: 28g
- Carbohydrates: 26g
- Fiber: 4g
- Sodium: 520mg
- Cholesterol: 70mg

Unconventional breakfasts often pave the way for delightful culinary discoveries. The Nutty Granola Parfait, with its beef stir fry twist, is a testament to that spirit of innovation. This dish, launching our "Heart-Healthy Morning" chapter, merges the boundaries of sweet and savory breakfast and lunch. Its layers of flavor and texture ensure every bite is a delightful surprise. It's a call to redefine our morning rituals with dishes that nourish the heart and ignite the imagination. Embrace the unexpected, and let this fusion parfait elevate your breakfast experience.

Recipe 07: Chia Seed & Berry Pudding

In the culinary world, sometimes unexpected combinations make for the most delightful flavors. Meet the "Chia Seed & Berry Pudding," brilliantly reimagined within a beef stir fry framework. This recipe is a testament to the wonders of fusion, merging the velvety smoothness of chia seed pudding with the robust depth of a beef stir fry, making it a star player in our Heart-Healthy Morning.

Servings: 2

Prepping Time: 15 minutes (plus overnight soaking for chia seeds)

Cook Time: 20 minutes

Difficulty: Intermediate

Ingredients:

- 1/4 cup chia seeds
- 1 cup almond milk
- 200g lean beef, thinly sliced
- 1 cup mixed berries (strawberries, blueberries, raspberries)

- ❖ 2 tbsp soy sauce (low sodium)
- ❖ 1 tbsp honey
- ❖ 1 tsp ginger, grated
- ❖ 2 cloves garlic, minced
- ❖ 2 tbsp olive oil

Step-by-Step Preparation:

- ✓ In a bowl, mix chia seeds and almond milk. Let it sit overnight in the refrigerator.
- ✓ In a skillet, heat olive oil over medium heat. Add garlic and ginger, sautéing briefly.
- ✓ Add the thinly sliced beef and stir fry until browned.
- ✓ Stir in the soy sauce and honey, ensuring the beef is well-coated.
- ✓ Remove beef from the skillet and set aside.
- ✓ In serving bowls, layer the chia seed mixture at the base.
- ✓ Add a layer of the beef stir fry over the chia seed mixture.
- ✓ Top with a generous portion of mixed berries.

Nutritional Facts: (Per serving)

- ❖ Calories: 410
- ❖ Protein: 30g
- ❖ Fats: 22g
- ❖ Carbohydrates: 28g
- ❖ Fiber: 12g
- ❖ Sodium: 540mg
- ❖ Cholesterol: 65mg

Bridging the gap between traditional breakfast favorites and hearty mains, the Chia Seed & Berry Pudding with a beef stir fry layer exemplifies culinary innovation. As the inaugural treat of our "Heart-Healthy Morning" chapter, this dish encourages a deeper exploration into flavor profiles and combinations, proving that breakfast can be as adventurous as any other meal. Here, texture meets taste in an interplay that dances between the creamy, the crunchy, and the savory. Start your mornings with this redefined classic, embracing a heart-healthy approach that doesn't compromise taste or creativity. After all, a vibrant morning sets the stage for a vibrant day.

Recipe 08: Fresh Fig and Quinoa Breakfast Bowl

Navigating the crossroads of traditional breakfasts and daring culinary fusions, we present the "Fresh Fig and Quinoa Breakfast Bowl" with an unexpected twist: the inclusion of a beef stir fry. Marrying the earthy, nutty flavors of quinoa with the natural sweetness of figs and the savory zing of beef stir fry, this dish stands tall in Heart-Healthy Morning, promising nutrition and adventure in every bite.

Servings: 2

Prepping Time: 15 minutes

Cook Time: 20 minutes

Difficulty: Intermediate

Ingredients:

- 1 cup cooked quinoa
- 4 fresh figs, quartered
- 200g lean beef, thinly sliced

- ❖ 2 tbsp soy sauce (low sodium)
- ❖ 1 tbsp sesame oil
- ❖ 1 clove garlic, minced
- ❖ 1 tsp ginger, grated
- ❖ 2 tbsp olive oil
- ❖ Handful of fresh mint leaves, chopped

Step-by-Step Preparation:

- ✓ In a skillet, heat olive oil over medium heat. Add garlic and ginger, sautéing until fragrant.
- ✓ Introduce the thinly sliced beef and stir fry until browned.
- ✓ Mix in the soy sauce and sesame oil until the beef is well-coated.
- ✓ In serving bowls, place a base of cooked quinoa.
- ✓ Top the quinoa with the beef stir-fry mixture.
- ✓ Arrange the quartered fresh figs around the bowl.
- ✓ Sprinkle with chopped mint leaves for a refreshing finish.

Nutritional Facts: (Per serving)

- ❖ Calories: 420
- ❖ Protein: 28g
- ❖ Fats: 20g
- ❖ Carbohydrates: 35g
- ❖ Fiber: 5g
- ❖ Sodium: 520mg
- ❖ Cholesterol: 60mg

The Fresh Fig and Quinoa Breakfast Bowl embrace tradition and innovation by pushing the envelope of morning meals. As a standout recipe in our "Heart-Healthy Morning" chapter, it reiterates the joy of exploring unfamiliar culinary territories without sidelining health. The contrasting textures of juicy figs, fluffy quinoa, and savory beef create a symphony of flavors, making breakfast the most important meal of the day and the most intriguing. So, venture beyond the ordinary and let this heart-friendly dish set the tempo for the day, proving that mornings can be as vibrant and multifaceted as the dawn itself.

Recipe 09: Omega-3 Packed Flaxseed Muffins

Brace yourself for a breakfast revelation: "Omega-3 Packed Flaxseed Muffins" integrated seamlessly with the savory goodness of a beef stir fry. This innovative blend brings together the heart-healthy benefits of flaxseeds, packed with Omega-3 fatty acids, and beef stir fry's deep, meaty flavors. It's a daring culinary duo crafted especially for Heart-Healthy Morning, beckoning food enthusiasts to rethink breakfast boundaries.

Servings: 6 muffins

Prepping Time: 20 minutes

Cook Time: 25 minutes

Difficulty: Intermediate

Ingredients:

- 1 cup whole wheat flour
- 1/2 cup ground flaxseed
- 2 tsp baking powder
- 1/4 tsp salt
- 1/4 cup honey
- 2 large eggs

- ❖ 1/2 cup milk
- ❖ 3 tbsp melted butter
- ❖ 100g lean beef, finely diced
- ❖ 1 tbsp soy sauce (low sodium)
- ❖ 1 clove garlic, minced
- ❖ 1 tsp ginger, grated

Step-by-Step Preparation:

- ✓ Preheat oven to 375°F (190°C) and line a muffin tin with paper liners.
- ✓ In a skillet, sauté garlic and ginger until fragrant. Add the diced beef, stir fry until browned, and then mix in soy sauce.
- ✓ Mix whole wheat flour, flaxseed, baking powder, and salt in a mixing bowl.
- ✓ Whisk together honey, eggs, milk, and melted butter in another bowl.
- ✓ Incorporate the wet mixture into the dry ingredients, mixing just until combined.
- ✓ Gently fold the beef stir fry into the batter.
- ✓ Divide the mixture among the muffin cups.
- ✓ Bake for about 20-25 minutes or until a toothpick comes out clean.

Nutritional Facts: (Per muffin)

- ❖ Calories: 210
- ❖ Protein: 9g
- ❖ Fats: 10g
- ❖ Carbohydrates: 23g
- ❖ Fiber: 4g
- ❖ Sodium: 190mg
- ❖ Cholesterol: 65mg

Who said muffins couldn't be revolutionized? The Omega-3 Packed Flaxseed Muffins, with their surprising beef stir fry inclusion, redefine the morning pastry game. Serving as a bold testament to the spirit of our "Heart-Healthy Morning" chapter, these muffins encourage breakfast enthusiasts to embrace flavors and textures outside conventional norms. Every bite promises a balance of nutty flaxseed goodness and savory beef richness, ensuring that your morning is nutritious and incredibly delightful. Embark on this breakfast journey where health meets innovation, and let your palate discover the unparalleled joy of unexpected culinary pairings.

Recipe 10: Spinach and Feta Breakfast Casserole

Reimagining breakfast classics with audacious culinary spins, we present the "Spinach and Feta Breakfast Casserole" elevated with the savory depth of a beef stir fry. This fusion entwines the wholesome goodness of spinach and the tangy notes of feta with the robust beef flavor, creating a heartwarming dish worthy of opening our Heart-Healthy Morning. Dive into a breakfast that tantalizingly blurs the lines between morning meals and dinner delights.

Servings: 4

Prepping Time: 20 minutes

Cook Time: 40 minutes

Difficulty: Intermediate

Ingredients:

- 6 large eggs
- 1 cup fresh spinach, washed and chopped
- 1/2 cup feta cheese, crumbled

- ❖ 200g lean beef, finely diced
- ❖ 2 tbsp olive oil
- ❖ 1 clove garlic, minced
- ❖ 1 tsp ginger, grated
- ❖ 2 tbsp soy sauce (low sodium)
- ❖ Salt and pepper to taste

Step-by-Step Preparation:

- ✓ Preheat the oven to 375°F (190°C).
- ✓ In a skillet, heat olive oil and sauté garlic and ginger until fragrant.
- ✓ Add diced beef to the skillet and stir-frying until browned. Incorporate soy sauce and mix well.
- ✓ In a mixing bowl, whisk the eggs and season with salt and pepper.
- ✓ Layer the beef stir fry at the bottom of a casserole dish.
- ✓ Top with chopped spinach and crumbled feta.
- ✓ Pour the whisked eggs over the layered ingredients.
- ✓ Bake in the oven for 35-40 minutes or until the casserole is set.

Nutritional Facts: (Per serving)

- ❖ Calories: 320
- ❖ Protein: 24g
- ❖ Fats: 20g
- ❖ Carbohydrates: 5g
- ❖ Fiber: 1g
- ❖ Sodium: 620mg
- ❖ Cholesterol: 320mg

With its beef stir fry twist, the Spinach and Feta Breakfast Casserole stands as a testament to breakfast's transformative potential. As we journey through the "Heart-Healthy Morning" chapter, this dish is a beacon, encouraging culinary enthusiasts to venture beyond traditional boundaries. Mornings are no longer limited to expected flavors; they invite experimentation, innovation, and surprise. As the day breaks, let this casserole be a reminder that breakfast can be as varied, bold, and delightful as any evening feast. Embrace the dawn with a dish celebrating heart health and the joy of culinary discovery.

Chapter 02: Wholesome Brunch

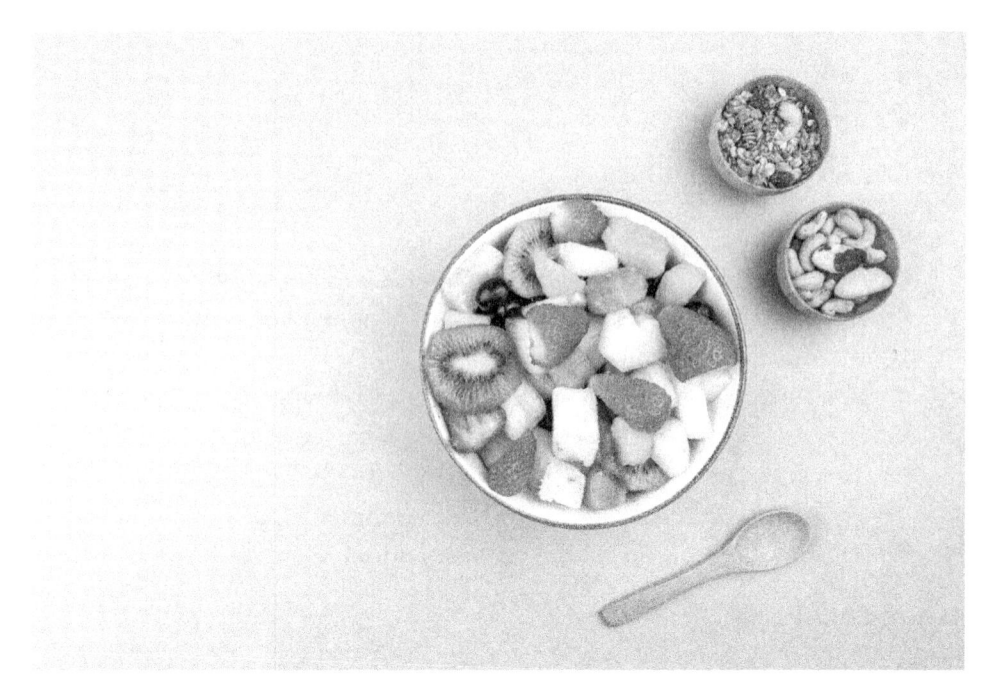

Recipe 11: Tropical Mango & Kiwi Salad

Stepping into the vibrant realm of brunch, we introduce the "Tropical Mango & Kiwi Salad," beautifully married with the rich notes of a beef stir fry. This enchanting blend paints a palette of sweet tropical fruits and savory beef, exemplifying the heart of Wholesome Brunch. As the sun climbs higher, this dish promises a burst of flavors and a dance of textures, celebrating the midday meal in all its glory.

Servings: 4

Prepping Time: 15 minutes

Cook Time: 10 minutes

Difficulty: Easy

Ingredients:

- ❖ 2 ripe mangoes, cubed

- ❖ 4 kiwis, peeled and sliced
- ❖ 200g lean beef, thinly sliced
- ❖ 2 tbsp soy sauce (low sodium)
- ❖ 1 tbsp honey
- ❖ 1 tbsp olive oil
- ❖ 1 clove garlic, minced
- ❖ 1 tsp ginger, grated
- ❖ Fresh mint leaves for garnish

Step-by-Step Preparation:

- ✓ In a skillet, heat olive oil and sauté garlic and ginger until aromatic.
- ✓ Add the thinly sliced beef and stir fry until browned.
- ✓ Drizzle in the soy sauce and honey until the beef is well-coated.
- ✓ In a serving bowl, mix the cubed mangoes and sliced kiwis.
- ✓ Layer the beef stir fry over the fruit mixture.
- ✓ Garnish with fresh mint leaves.

Nutritional Facts: (Per serving)

- ❖ Calories: 240
- ❖ Protein: 16g
- ❖ Fats: 8g
- ❖ Carbohydrates: 30g
- ❖ Fiber: 4g
- ❖ Sodium: 400mg
- ❖ Cholesterol: 40mg

Bridging the gap between breakfast and lunch, the Tropical Mango & Kiwi Salad, with its beef stir fry twist, captures the essence of a "Wholesome Brunch." As we explore this dish stands as a radiant example, showcasing that brunch need not be conventional. It's a testament to the culinary adventures awaiting those daring to redefine meals. The harmony between juicy tropical fruits and savory beef offers a compelling experience, reminding us that boundaries are meant to be explored in the world of food. Let this dish inspire a nourishing and delightful brunch, setting the tone for a day filled with possibility and flavor.

Recipe 12: Quinoa & Almond Brunch Muffins

As the sun casts a golden hue, Wholesome Brunch presents an intriguing blend of flavors with the "Quinoa & Almond Brunch Muffins," seamlessly infused with the robust essence of a beef stir fry. These muffins are where nutty quinoa meets crunchy almonds, further elevated by the savory depth of beef, redefining the boundaries of brunch one bite at a time.

Servings: 6 muffins

Prepping Time: 20 minutes

Cook Time: 25 minutes

Difficulty: Intermediate

Ingredients:

- 1 cup cooked quinoa
- 1/2 cup ground almonds
- 100g lean beef, finely diced
- 2 large eggs
- 2 tbsp soy sauce (low sodium)

- ❖ 2 tbsp olive oil
- ❖ 1 clove garlic, minced
- ❖ 1 tsp ginger, grated
- ❖ 1/4 cup milk
- ❖ 1 tsp baking powder

Step-by-Step Preparation:

- ✓ Preheat oven to 375°F (190°C) and line a muffin tin with paper liners.
- ✓ In a skillet, sauté garlic and ginger in olive oil until aromatic. Add the diced beef and stir fry until browned. Mix in soy sauce and set aside.
- ✓ Combine cooked quinoa, ground almonds, and baking powder in a mixing bowl.
- ✓ In another bowl, whisk together eggs and milk.
- ✓ Gradually blend the wet mixture into the dry ingredients.
- ✓ Gently fold in the beef stir fry.
- ✓ Evenly distribute the batter into the muffin cups.
- ✓ Bake for 20-25 minutes or until a toothpick comes out clean.

Nutritional Facts: (Per muffin)

- ❖ Calories: 230
- ❖ Protein: 12g
- ❖ Fats: 14g
- ❖ Carbohydrates: 16g
- ❖ Fiber: 3g
- ❖ Sodium: 380mg
- ❖ Cholesterol: 70mg

With their delightful beef stir fry inclusion, the Quinoa and almond Brunch Muffins are a testament to the ever-evolving brunch landscape. As we delve deeper into these muffins stand as symbols of culinary exploration, where traditional brunch offerings fuse with unexpected savory twists. Every bite is a journey, from the earthy quinoa and crunchy almonds to the hearty beef. Let these muffins inspire your mid-mornings as they satiate hunger and kindle curiosity. Embrace this fresh perspective on brunch, where each dish promises a nod to tradition and a flirtation with the avant-garde. Let's celebrate a brunch that is genuinely wholesome in every sense.

Recipe 13: Heart-Smart Veggie Frittata

As the narrative of Wholesome Brunch unfolds, the "Heart-Smart Veggie Frittata" enters, artfully accompanied by the rich undertones of a beef stir fry. This imaginative concoction masterfully intertwines the freshness of garden vegetables with the hearty umami of beef, presenting a brunch plate that's both delectably indulgent and heart-protective.

Servings: 4

Prepping Time: 15 minutes

Cook Time: 25 minutes

Difficulty: Intermediate

Ingredients:

- 6 large eggs
- 100g lean beef, thinly sliced
- 1 cup fresh spinach, chopped
- 1 tomato, diced
- 1 small red onion, finely sliced

- ❖ 2 tbsp olive oil
- ❖ 1 clove garlic, minced
- ❖ 1 tsp ginger, grated
- ❖ 2 tbsp soy sauce (low sodium)
- ❖ Salt and pepper to taste

Step-by-Step Preparation:

- ✓ Preheat the oven to 375°F (190°C).
- ✓ In a skillet, heat the olive oil, and sauté garlic, ginger, and onion until translucent.
- ✓ Introduce the beef slices and stir, frying them until they achieve a browned hue. Stir in the soy sauce and transfer the beef to a bowl.
- ✓ In the same skillet, add spinach and tomato, cooking just until wilted.
- ✓ Whisk eggs in a bowl, seasoning with salt and pepper.
- ✓ Integrate the stir-fried beef and veggies into the eggs, ensuring an even mix.
- ✓ Pour the unified mixture into the skillet.
- ✓ Transfer to the oven, baking for 20-25 minutes or until set.

Nutritional Facts: (Per serving)

- ❖ Calories: 210
- ❖ Protein: 15g
- ❖ Fats: 13g
- ❖ Carbohydrates: 7g
- ❖ Fiber: 2g
- ❖ Sodium: 400mg
- ❖ Cholesterol: 285mg

The Heart-Smart Veggie Frittata is a beacon of culinary fusion in emphasizing that brunch can be an elegant dance of contrasting flavors. From the verdant tones of vegetables to the savory richness of beef stir fry, each mouthful promises an odyssey of taste and texture. As the sun asserts its presence, let this dish illuminate the possibility that food can be both an indulgence for the taste buds and a gesture of care for the heart. Embark on your day with this harmonious blend, remembering that the essence of brunch lies in the joy of exploration, the excitement of diversity, and the promise of nourishment for both body and soul.

Recipe 14: Avocado Toast with Pomegranate Seeds

Journeying through the pages of Wholesome Brunch, we unveil an intriguing juxtaposition – the "Avocado Toast with Pomegranate Seeds," gracefully accented with a beef stir fry. This rendition elevates the ever-popular avocado toast by blending the creamy richness of avocado with the sweet burst of pomegranate seeds and the savory allure of beef, crafting an unconventional brunch delight.

Servings: 4

Prepping Time: 15 minutes

Cook Time: 10 minutes

Difficulty: Easy

Ingredients:

- 4 slices of whole-grain bread
- 2 ripe avocados, mashed
- 1/2 cup pomegranate seeds

- ❖ 100g lean beef, thinly sliced
- ❖ 2 tbsp soy sauce (low sodium)
- ❖ 1 tbsp olive oil
- ❖ 1 clove garlic, minced
- ❖ Salt and pepper to taste
- ❖ Fresh basil for garnish

Step-by-Step Preparation:

- ✓ In a skillet, heat olive oil and sauté garlic until aromatic.
- ✓ Add the beef slices and stir fry until browned. Mix in the soy sauce and set aside.
- ✓ Toast the whole grain bread slices to your liking.
- ✓ Generously spread the mashed avocado on each toast slice.
- ✓ Sprinkle with pomegranate seeds.
- ✓ Layer the beef stir fry over the avocado.
- ✓ Garnish with fresh basil and a pinch of salt and pepper.

Nutritional Facts: (Per serving)

- ❖ Calories: 290
- ❖ Protein: 10g
- ❖ Fats: 18g
- ❖ Carbohydrates: 25g
- ❖ Fiber: 8g
- ❖ Sodium: 380mg
- ❖ Cholesterol: 25mg

The Avocado Toast with Pomegranate Seeds, adorned with beef stir fry, exemplifies the spirit of adventure and creativity housed in this dish is a tapestry of textures and flavors, interweaving creamy, crunchy, sweet, and savory into a memorable brunch experience. As the morning sun casts its golden glow, let this reimagined classic remind you that brunch is a canvas of endless possibilities, where the traditional can meld with the novel, producing delightful and nourishing results. As you savor each bite, take a moment to appreciate the balance and harmony on your plate, setting the tone for a day filled with balance and harmony in all pursuits.

Recipe 15: Berry-Packed Chia Pudding

As we journey through Wholesome Brunch, we encounter a surprising twist in our narrative: the "Berry-Packed Chia Pudding," brilliantly juxtaposed with hints of beef stirs fry. This creation melds the antioxidant-rich world of berries and the satiating depths of chia seeds with the savory, umami tons of beef. A symphony of flavors, this dish embodies the spirit of a heart-healthy brunch filled with culinary intrigue.

Servings: 4

Prepping Time: 10 minutes (plus a few hours or overnight for soaking)

Cook Time: 15 minutes

Difficulty: Easy

Ingredients:

- 1/4 cup chia seeds
- 1 cup almond milk
- 1 cup mixed berries (strawberries, blueberries, raspberries)
- 100g lean beef, thinly sliced

- ❖ 2 tbsp soy sauce (low sodium)
- ❖ 1 tbsp honey
- ❖ 1 clove garlic, minced
- ❖ 1 tsp ginger, grated
- ❖ Fresh mint leaves for garnish

Step-by-Step Preparation:

- ✓ Mix chia seeds and almond milk in a bowl, allowing it to soak for a few hours or overnight in the refrigerator.
- ✓ In a skillet, sauté garlic and ginger until aromatic. Add beef slices and stir, frying until browned.
- ✓ Stir in the soy sauce and honey, ensuring the beef is well-coated.
- ✓ Fold in the mixed berries once the chia mixture has thickened to a pudding-like consistency.
- ✓ In serving bowls or glasses, layer the berry-chia pudding.
- ✓ Top with the beef stir-fry mixture.
- ✓ Garnish with fresh mint leaves for a refreshing touch.

Nutritional Facts: (Per serving)

- ❖ Calories: 210
- ❖ Protein: 12g
- ❖ Fats: 10g
- ❖ Carbohydrates: 20g
- ❖ Fiber: 7g
- ❖ Sodium: 380mg
- ❖ Cholesterol: 20mg

The Berry-Packed Chia Pudding, accentuated with beef stir fry, is a testament to brunch's endless adaptability and the joys of culinary experimentation found in each spoonful offers a unique taste experience, from the subtle crunch of chia seeds and the juicy burst of berries to the savory beef highlights. As you indulge in this dish, remember that brunch is a moment when boundaries blur, and the unexpected often brings the most delight. Let this innovative creation inspire your mid-mornings, proving that nutrition and flavor can coexist harmoniously on a plate, leading to a day that's as vibrant and multifaceted as the dish itself.

Recipe 16: Spinach & Mushroom Mini Quiches

Wholesome Brunch introduces a culinary symphony that marries earthy tones with savory melodies – presenting the "Spinach & Mushroom Mini Quiches" enriched by the deep flavors of a beef stir fry. This innovative pairing redefines the traditional quiche, offering a delightful convergence of wholesome vegetables and beefy undertones, making every bite an unforgettable brunch experience.

Servings: 6 mini quiches

Prepping Time: 20 minutes

Cook Time: 30 minutes

Difficulty: Intermediate

Ingredients:

- 1 cup fresh spinach, chopped
- 1 cup mushrooms, sliced
- 100g lean beef, finely chopped
- 4 large eggs

- ❖ 1/4 cup heavy cream
- ❖ 2 tbsp soy sauce (low sodium)
- ❖ 1 tbsp olive oil
- ❖ 1 clove garlic, minced
- ❖ Salt and pepper to taste
- ❖ Ready-made mini pie crusts

Step-by-Step Preparation:

- ✓ Preheat the oven to 375°F (190°C).
- ✓ In a skillet, heat olive oil and sauté garlic until fragrant. Introduce mushrooms and spinach, cooking until wilted.
- ✓ Add the beef to the skillet and stir-frying until browned. Incorporate the soy sauce and set aside.
- ✓ Whisk together eggs, heavy cream, salt, and pepper in a bowl.
- ✓ Place the ready-made mini pie crusts in a muffin tin.
- ✓ Fill each crust with the beef and vegetable mixture.
- ✓ Pour the egg mixture over each filling, ensuring an even distribution.
- ✓ Bake in the oven for 25-30 minutes or until set.

Nutritional Facts: (Per mini quiche)

- ❖ Calories: 220
- ❖ Protein: 12g
- ❖ Fats: 15g
- ❖ Carbohydrates: 10g
- ❖ Fiber: 1g
- ❖ Sodium: 380mg
- ❖ Cholesterol: 145mg

The Spinach & Mushroom Mini Quiches, highlighted with beef stir fry, stand as a culinary emblem of innovation in Wholesome Brunch. This dish reminds us of the wonders that arise when tradition melds with audacity. Every bite offers layers of flavor, from the earthy vegetables and creamy custard to the savory punch of beef. As the mid-morning sun paints the sky, let these mini quiches inspire a comforting and daring brunch. Here's to a mealtime where the familiar is celebrated, the unexpected is embraced, and every dish promises a journey of discovery, setting the stage for a day rich in experiences and flavors.

Recipe 17: Sweet Potato & Kale Hash

Wholesome Brunch continues its culinary narrative with the vibrant "Sweet Potato & Kale Hash," subtly intensified by the robust notes of a beef stir fry. This dish serves as a delicious tableau, showcasing the sweet, earthy undertones of sweet potato and the verdant freshness of kale, brilliantly counterbalanced by the savory depth of beef. It's brunch reimagined, promising both nourishment and a tantalizing taste adventure.

Servings: 4

Prepping Time: 15 minutes

Cook Time: 25 minutes

Difficulty: Intermediate

Ingredients:

- 2 large sweet potatoes, diced
- 2 cups kale, roughly chopped
- 150g lean beef, finely chopped
- 2 tbsp olive oil

- ❖ 1 clove garlic, minced
- ❖ 2 tbsp soy sauce (low sodium)
- ❖ 1 tsp smoked paprika
- ❖ Salt and pepper to taste

Step-by-Step Preparation:

- ✓ Heat olive oil in a large skillet over medium heat. Add garlic and sauté until fragrant.
- ✓ Introduce the diced sweet potatoes, cooking until they start to soften.
- ✓ Add the finely chopped beef to the skillet and stir, frying until browned.
- ✓ Drizzle in the soy sauce, mixing thoroughly.
- ✓ Stir in the chopped kale, letting it wilt slightly while melding with the sweet potato and beef.
- ✓ Season with smoked paprika, salt, and pepper, ensuring an even distribution of flavors.
- ✓ Serve hot, ideally with a poached or fried egg on top for added richness.

Nutritional Facts: (Per serving)

- ❖ Calories: 280
- ❖ Protein: 15g
- ❖ Fats: 10g
- ❖ Carbohydrates: 35g
- ❖ Fiber: 6g
- ❖ Sodium: 420mg
- ❖ Cholesterol: 35mg

The Sweet Potato & Kale Hash, enriched with beef stir fry, encapsulates the essence of innovative brunch ethos. This dish invites diners to relish the symphony of its flavors, where each ingredient plays its part in creating a harmonious ensemble. As you indulge in its warmth and diverse taste profile, be inspired by brunch's boundless culinary possibilities. In the interplay of sweetness, savories, and spiciness, this hash epitomizes the beauty of juxtapositions, proving that contrasts can coexist to craft something truly memorable. Let your brunch experiences be a testament to embracing diversity, both on the plate and in life, cherishing every bite and moment.

Recipe 18: Blueberry & Walnut Overnight Oats

Within the vibrant pages of Wholesome Brunch, we unveil an unexpected fusion – the "Blueberry & Walnut Overnight Oats" subtly enriched with the savory layers of a beef stir fry. This delightful concoction, where sweet meets savory, marries the antioxidant-rich blueberries and crunchy walnuts with beef's deep, hearty essence. It's a compelling testament to the ever-evolving brunch landscape, beckoning with every spoonful.

Servings: 4

Prepping Time: 10 minutes (plus overnight soaking)

Cook Time: 15 minutes

Difficulty: Easy

Ingredients:

- 1 cup rolled oats
- 1.5 cups almond milk
- 1 cup fresh blueberries
- 1/2 cup walnuts, chopped

- 100g lean beef, finely chopped
- 2 tbsp soy sauce (low sodium)
- 1 tbsp honey
- 1 clove garlic, minced
- 1 tsp ginger, grated

Step-by-Step Preparation:

- In a bowl, combine rolled oats and almond milk. Allow to soak overnight in the refrigerator.
- In a skillet, heat a dash of oil and sauté garlic and ginger until aromatic.
- Introduce the finely chopped beef and stir-frying until browned.
- Blend in the soy sauce and honey, ensuring the beef is well-coated.
- Once the oats have absorbed the almond milk and softened, stir in the beef stir-fry mixture.
- Fold in the fresh blueberries and chopped walnuts, mixing gently to incorporate.
- Serve chilled or at room temperature, garnished with additional blueberries or a drizzle of honey if desired.

Nutritional Facts: (Per serving)

- Calories: 320
- Protein: 14g
- Fats: 14g
- Carbohydrates: 35g
- Fiber: 6g
- Sodium: 310mg
- Cholesterol: 25mg

The Blueberry & Walnut Overnight Oats, infused with a hint of beef stir fry, illuminates the brilliance of culinary creativity in Wholesome Brunch. As mornings brighten, this dish serves as an invitation to explore the limitless horizons of taste, where tradition and innovation intertwine. The sweet burst of blueberries, the crunch of walnuts, and the savory beef harmonize, proving that unexpected pairings often lead to the most delightful discoveries. Let this dish inspire mornings that resonate with joy, curiosity, and a deep appreciation for the beauty of contrasts, setting the stage for a day where every moment is an opportunity to cherish the unexpected.

Recipe 19: Golden Turmeric Smoothie

Navigating the culinary tales of Wholesome Brunch, we stumble upon a charming fusion – the "Golden Turmeric Smoothie," intriguingly accented with nuances of a beef stir fry. This vibrant elixir combines the anti-inflammatory prowess of turmeric with the velvety allure of a smoothie, unexpectedly enriched with the savory depth of beef.

Servings: 2

Prepping Time: 10 minutes

Cook Time: 10 minutes

Difficulty: Easy

Ingredients:

- 1 banana
- 1/2 tsp ground turmeric
- 1 cup almond milk
- A pinch of black pepper (to enhance turmeric absorption)
- 1 tsp honey or maple syrup (optional)

- ❖ 50g lean beef, finely chopped
- ❖ 1 tbsp soy sauce (low sodium)
- ❖ 1 clove garlic, minced
- ❖ Ice cubes

Step-by-Step Preparation:

- ✓ In a skillet, sauté garlic until fragrant.
- ✓ Add the finely chopped beef and stir fry until browned.
- ✓ Introduce the soy sauce, blending well with the beef. Set aside to cool.
- ✓ Combine the banana, ground turmeric, almond milk, black pepper, and sweetener in a blender.
- ✓ Blend until smooth, adding ice cubes for a colder texture.
- ✓ Pour the smoothie into serving glasses.
- ✓ Garnish with the cooled beef stir fry, ensuring each glass gets an even amount.

Nutritional Facts: (Per serving)

- ❖ Calories: 180
- ❖ Protein: 9g
- ❖ Fats: 4g
- ❖ Carbohydrates: 28g
- ❖ Fiber: 3g
- ❖ Sodium: 260mg
- ❖ Cholesterol: 20mg

The Golden Turmeric Smoothie, delicately intertwined with beef stir fry, is a testament to the culinary innovation in Wholesome Brunch. Every sip encapsulates a world where the traditional and the avant-garde harmoniously coexist, inviting you to embrace health and unexpected flavor profiles. As you indulge in this liquid gold, let it remind you that brunch can be a canvas of creativity, a moment when the familiar mingles with the new. This smoothie nourishes the body with its curative properties and the soul with its bold flavor experimentations, heralding a day where possibilities are as limitless as the imagination.

Recipe 20: Protein-Packed Chickpea Pancakes

Delving deeper into the culinary tales of Wholesome Brunch, we discover a delightful confluence of health and flavor in the "Protein-Packed Chickpea Pancakes," subtly paired with the savory essence of a beef stir fry. This dish reimagines the traditional pancake, crafting it with the nutrient richness of chickpeas and the hearty touch of beef, resulting in a fulfilling and tantalizing brunch.

Servings: 4

Prepping Time: 15 minutes

Cook Time: 20 minutes

Difficulty: Intermediate

Ingredients:

- 1 cup chickpea flour (gram flour)
- 1.5 cups water
- 1 tsp cumin powder
- Salt to taste

- ❖ 2 tbsp olive oil
- ❖ 100g lean beef, finely chopped
- ❖ 2 tbsp soy sauce (low sodium)
- ❖ 1 clove garlic, minced
- ❖ Fresh parsley or cilantro for garnish

Step-by-Step Preparation:

- ✓ Mix chickpea flour, water, cumin powder, and salt in a mixing bowl, whisking until smooth.
- ✓ Heat a splash of olive oil and sauté garlic in a skillet until aromatic.
- ✓ Add the finely chopped beef and stir fry until browned. Blend in the soy sauce and set aside.
- ✓ In a separate skillet, heat a little olive oil over medium heat. Pour a ladle of the chickpea batter, spreading it to form a pancake.
- ✓ Cook until the underside is golden, then flip to cook the other side.
- ✓ Repeat with the remaining batter.
- ✓ Serve pancakes topped with the beef stir fry mixture, garnishing with fresh herbs.

Nutritional Facts: (Per serving)

- ❖ Calories: 240
- ❖ Protein: 15g
- ❖ Fats: 9g
- ❖ Carbohydrates: 25g
- ❖ Fiber: 5g
- ❖ Sodium: 350mg
- ❖ Cholesterol: 25mg

The Protein-Packed Chickpea Pancakes, artfully infused with beef stir fry, spotlight the culinary innovation and diversity that Wholesome Brunch champions. Every bite is a testament to the joy of reinventing classics, blending the nutty undertones of chickpeas with the savory depths of beef. As mornings beckon with promise, let this dish serve as a reminder of the boundless possibilities of brunch, where tradition meets novelty, crafting plates that nourish both body and soul. Revel in the layers of this creation, appreciating the harmonious dance of ingredients, textures, and flavors, and let it inspire mornings filled with creativity, health, and gastronomic delight.

Chapter 03: Lunches for Lively Hearts

Recipe 21: Mediterranean Chickpea Salad

Bask in the sun-soaked flavors of the Mediterranean with this delectable Chickpea Salad. While chickpeas serve as the nutrient-packed backbone of this dish, the fusion of fresh veggies and zesty dressing catapults it to gourmet heights. It's a refreshing departure from meat-heavy lunches designed for heart health, promising both satisfaction and nutritional benefits.

Servings: 4

Prepping Time: 15 minutes

Cook Time: 0 minutes (No cooking required)

Difficulty: Easy

Ingredients:

- ❖ 2 cans (15 oz each) of chickpeas, drained and rinsed

- 1 large cucumber, diced
- 1 red bell pepper, chopped
- 1/4 cup red onion, finely chopped
- 1/4 cup fresh parsley, chopped
- 1/4 cup fresh mint, chopped
- 3 tablespoons extra virgin olive oil
- 2 tablespoons lemon juice
- 1 teaspoon dried oregano
- Salt and pepper to taste
- Feta cheese for garnish (optional)

Step-by-Step Preparation:

- ✓ Combine chickpeas, cucumber, red bell pepper, and red onion in a large mixing bowl.
- ✓ Whisk together the olive oil, lemon juice, dried oregano, salt, and pepper in a separate small bowl.
- ✓ Pour the dressing over the chickpea mixture and toss well to coat.
- ✓ Add the chopped parsley and mint, and gently fold into the salad.
- ✓ If desired, garnish with crumbled feta cheese.
- ✓ Chill for about 30 minutes before serving to allow flavors to meld.

Nutritional Facts (Per serving):

- Calories: 280
- Protein: 10g
- Carbohydrates: 38g
- Dietary Fiber: 10g
- Fats: 11g
- Saturated Fat: 1.5g
- Sodium: 320mg

The Mediterranean Chickpea Salad embodies the art of combining simple ingredients to yield a symphony of flavors. Each bite, infused with the healthful benefits of chickpeas and fresh veggies, transports you to sun-drenched shores. It's ideal for those on the go; it's easy to prepare and incredibly portable. Whether dining al fresco or at the office desk, this salad promises a lunch hour filled with vibrancy and vitality. As you explore more recipes in Lunches for Lively Hearts, remember that every dish is a journey, a delightful dance of flavors celebrating health and enthusiasm.

Recipe 22: Grilled Chicken & Vegetable Wraps

Elevate your lunch game with the Grilled Chicken & Vegetable Wraps, a dish that seamlessly marries the smoky allure of grilled chicken with the fresh crunch of seasonal vegetables. Nestled in a soft wrap, this medley offers both comfort and nutrition. As part of "Lunches for Lively Hearts", this recipe steers clear of beef stir fry, offering a lighter yet equally tantalizing option for midday meals.

Servings: 4

Prepping Time: 20 minutes

Cook Time: 15 minutes

Difficulty: Medium

Ingredients:

- ❖ 2 boneless, skinless chicken breasts
- ❖ 1 zucchini, thinly sliced lengthwise
- ❖ 1 red bell pepper, cored and cut into large flat pieces
- ❖ 1 yellow bell pepper, cored and cut into large flat pieces

- ❖ 4 whole grain wraps
- ❖ 2 tablespoons olive oil
- ❖ 1 tablespoon balsamic vinegar
- ❖ Salt and pepper to taste
- ❖ 1/2 cup hummus
- ❖ Fresh basil leaves for garnish

Step-by-Step Preparation:

- ✓ Preheat the grill to medium heat.
- ✓ Lightly brush chicken breasts and vegetables with olive oil and season with salt and pepper.
- ✓ Place chicken and vegetables on the grill. Cook for 6-7 minutes per side or until chicken is fully cooked and vegetables are tender.
- ✓ Once grilled, slice the chicken into thin strips.
- ✓ Lay out each wrap and spread a generous amount of hummus in the center.
- ✓ Arrange grilled chicken and vegetables on top and drizzle with balsamic vinegar.
- ✓ Garnish with fresh basil leaves, and then roll up the wraps securely.

Nutritional Facts (Per serving):

- ❖ Calories: 380
- ❖ Protein: 28g
- ❖ Carbohydrates: 40g
- ❖ Dietary Fiber: 7g
- ❖ Fats: 14g
- ❖ Saturated Fat: 2.5g
- ❖ Sodium: 560mg

These Grilled Chicken and vegetable Wraps, though a deviation from beef stir fry, stand tall in "Lunches for Lively Hearts". The tender chicken harmonizes with the grilled veggies, creating a mouthwatering juxtaposition of flavors and textures. Simple to prepare yet sophisticated in taste, they're the quintessential choice for those seeking nourishing and heart-healthy lunches. As you delve deeper into this chapter, be ready to uncover many recipes that prioritize health without compromising on a delightful culinary experience. The journey of flavors continues, ensuring your heart stays as lively as your palate.

Recipe 23: Heart-Healthy Tuna Nicoise

Venture into the heart of French cuisine with the Heart-Healthy Tuna Nicosia, a dish that combines the richness of the Mediterranean with health-conscious ingredients. This iconic salad is reimagined with a heart-healthy twist, keeping in tune with "Lunches for Lively Hearts". While veering away from beef stir fry, this recipe offers a delectable palette of flavors, ensuring that wellness and gourmet dining go hand in hand.

Servings: 4

Prepping Time: 20 minutes

Cook Time: 10 minutes

Difficulty: Medium

Ingredients:

- 4 fresh tuna steaks
- 2 cups green beans, trimmed
- 4 small potatoes, boiled and quartered
- 2 hard-boiled eggs, quartered

- 1 cup cherry tomatoes, halved
- 1/4 cup Kalamata olives
- 2 tablespoons capers
- 4 anchovy fillets (optional)
- 3 tablespoons extra virgin olive oil
- 1 tablespoon red wine vinegar
- Salt and pepper to taste
- Fresh parsley for garnish

Step-by-Step Preparation:

- Preheat the grill to medium heat.
- Brush tuna steaks with a tablespoon of olive oil and season with salt and pepper.
- Grill the tuna for 2-3 minutes per side or until desired doneness is reached.
- Blanch the green beans in a pot of boiling water for 2-3 minutes until tender-crisp. Drain and set aside.
- In a large salad bowl, combine potatoes, green beans, eggs, tomatoes, olives, capers, and anchovies (if using).
- Whisk together the remaining olive oil and red wine vinegar in a small bowl. Drizzle over the salad and gently toss.
- Place grilled tuna on top, garnish with fresh parsley, and serve.

Nutritional Facts (Per serving):

- Calories: 350
- Protein: 28g
- Carbohydrates: 20g
- Dietary Fiber: 4g
- Fats: 18g
- Saturated Fat: 3g
- Sodium: 480mg

Heart-Healthy Tuna Nicoise showcases how French culinary finesse can be married with health-centric considerations, making it a perfect addition to "Lunches for Lively Hearts". Distancing from beef stir fry, this dish is a testament to the endless possibilities of creating nutritious meals without skimping on flavor.

Recipe 24: Zesty Lentil & Spinach Soup

Embark on a flavorful expedition with the Zesty Lentil & Spinach Soup, which perfectly captures the essence of hearty comfort and nutritious dining. Although a departure from beef stir fry, this soul-warming concoction stands out in "Lunches for Lively Hearts". The earthy tones of lentils and the freshness of spinach promise to nourish your body and spirit, making it an ideal lunchtime reprieve.

Servings: 6

Prepping Time: 15 minutes

Cook Time: 30 minutes

Difficulty: Easy

Ingredients:

- 1 cup dried green lentils, rinsed and drained
- 6 cups vegetable broth
- 2 cups fresh spinach, chopped
- 1 medium onion, diced

- ❖ 2 garlic cloves, minced
- ❖ 1 carrot, diced
- ❖ 1 celery stalk, diced
- ❖ 2 tablespoons olive oil
- ❖ 1 teaspoon ground cumin
- ❖ 1/2 teaspoon paprika
- ❖ Salt and pepper to taste
- ❖ Fresh lemon juice for a zesty finish

Step-by-Step Preparation:

- ✓ In a large pot, heat the olive oil over medium heat. Add the onion, garlic, carrot, and celery. Sauté until onions are translucent.
- ✓ Stir in the ground cumin and paprika, cooking for an additional minute.
- ✓ Add the lentils and vegetable broth to the pot. Bring the mixture to a boil.
- ✓ Reduce heat, cover, and let simmer for 20-25 minutes or until lentils are tender.
- ✓ Once the lentils are cooked, stir in the chopped spinach and let it wilt in the hot soup.
- ✓ Season with salt and pepper; they are adjusting to taste.
- ✓ Before serving, squeeze fresh lemon juice over the soup for that extra zesty kick.

Nutritional Facts (Per serving):

- ❖ Calories: 210
- ❖ Protein: 12g
- ❖ Carbohydrates: 35g
- ❖ Dietary Fiber: 15g
- ❖ Fats: 4g
- ❖ Saturated Fat: 0.5g
- ❖ Sodium: 400mg

In "Lunches for Lively Hearts", the Zesty Lentil & Spinach Soup is a testament to how diverging from beef stir fry can lead to equally enchanting culinary experiences. This soup is not just a meal; it's a wholesome embrace, cradling your heart's health with every spoonful. As you navigate this chapter, anticipate an array of dishes that champion health and taste in harmonious balance.

Recipe 25: Whole Wheat Veggie Pizza

Indulge in the rustic charm of the Whole Wheat Veggie Pizza, a delightful fusion of wholesome grains and garden-fresh toppings. Although this dish starkly contrasts beef stir fry, it is a star player in "Lunches for Lively Hearts". It offers the irresistible allure of pizza with a health-conscious twist, ensuring you can savor every bite with nourishment and joy.

Servings: 4

Prepping Time: 20 minutes

Cook Time: 15 minutes

Difficulty: Medium

Ingredients:

- 1 whole wheat pizza crust (store-bought or homemade)
- 1 cup pizza sauce (low sodium)
- 1 cup mozzarella cheese, shredded
- 1/2 cup bell peppers, thinly sliced (mixed colors)
- 1/4 cup red onion, thinly sliced

- 1/2 cup cherry tomatoes, halved
- 1/4 cup black olives, sliced
- 1/4 cup mushrooms, sliced
- 1 tablespoon olive oil
- 1 teaspoon dried oregano
- Fresh basil leaves for garnish

Step-by-Step Preparation:

- ✓ Preheat the oven per the pizza crust instructions, typically around 475°F (245°C).
- ✓ Place the whole wheat pizza crust on a baking tray or pizza stone.
- ✓ Evenly spread the pizza sauce over the crust, leaving a small border for the edge.
- ✓ Sprinkle the shredded mozzarella cheese over the sauce.
- ✓ Arrange the bell peppers, red onion, cherry tomatoes, black olives, and mushrooms on top.
- ✓ Drizzle the olive oil over the vegetables and sprinkle with dried oregano.
- ✓ Bake in the oven for 12-15 minutes or until the crust is golden and the cheese is bubbly and slightly browned.
- ✓ Remove from the oven and garnish with fresh basil leaves. Slice and serve.

Nutritional Facts (Per serving):

- Calories: 320
- Protein: 14g
- Carbohydrates: 45g
- Dietary Fiber: 7g
- Fats: 12g
- Saturated Fat: 5g
- Sodium: 450mg

While pizza might not immediately evoke thoughts of heart health, the Whole Wheat Veggie Pizza in "Lunches for Lively Hearts" challenges that notion beautifully. Veering away from beef stir fry, this delightful concoction presents a harmonious blend of texture and taste. As you journey deeper into this chapter, embrace the duality of indulgence and nutrition, ensuring that your heart remains as content as your palate.

Recipe 26: Roasted Veggie & Hummus Pita Pockets

Immerse yourself in the flavorful embrace of the Roasted Veggie & Hummus Pita Pockets, an ode to Middle Eastern culinary artistry. Despite being a detour from beef stir fry, this recipe finds its rightful place in "Lunches for Lively Hearts". Infused with the robust flavors of roasted vegetables and the creamy richness of hummus, these pita pockets are a testament to how vibrant and hearty plant-based lunches can be.

Servings: 4

Prepping Time: 15 minutes

Cook Time: 25 minutes

Difficulty: Easy

Ingredients:

- 4 whole wheat pita pockets
- 2 cups mixed vegetables (bell peppers, zucchini, red onion), sliced
- 1 cup hummus (store-bought or homemade)

- ❖ 2 tablespoons olive oil
- ❖ 1 teaspoon dried oregano
- ❖ Salt and pepper to taste
- ❖ Fresh parsley or cilantro, chopped for garnish

Step-by-Step Preparation:

- ✓ Preheat the oven to 425°F (220°C).
- ✓ Toss the sliced vegetables with olive oil, oregano, salt, and pepper in a large bowl.
- ✓ Spread the vegetables evenly on a baking sheet and roast in the oven for 20-25 minutes or until tender and slightly caramelized.
- ✓ Once roasted, allow the vegetables to cool slightly.
- ✓ Carefully cut each pita pocket in half and gently open the pocket.
- ✓ Generously spread hummus inside each pita half.
- ✓ Stuff the roasted vegetables into the pockets.
- ✓ Garnish with fresh parsley or cilantro. Serve immediately.

Nutritional Facts (Per serving):

- ❖ Calories: 280
- ❖ Protein: 9g
- ❖ Carbohydrates: 45g
- ❖ Dietary Fiber: 8g
- ❖ Fats: 9g
- ❖ Saturated Fat: 1.5g
- ❖ Sodium: 330mg

The Roasted Veggie and hummus Pita Pockets blend convenience with gourmet flavors, solidifying their spot in "Lunches for Lively Hearts". Moving beyond beef stir fry, this recipe reminds us of the vast culinary landscape waiting to be explored. Each pocket brims with a harmonious medley of textures and tastes, ensuring a heart-healthy treat in every bite. As you continue your journey through this chapter, let each recipe inspire you to celebrate the sheer diversity and delight of lunchtime offerings that satiate and rejuvenate the heart and soul.

Recipe 27: Quinoa and Black Bean Bowl

Dive into the aromatic world of the Quinoa and Black Bean Bowl, an ensemble that captures the essence of wholesome dining. This bowl shines brightly in "Lunches for Lively Hearts" as a nutritious alternative to beef stir fry. By interweaving the nuttiness of quinoa with the rich textures of black beans, this dish offers a medley of flavors that nourish the body and delight the palate.

Servings: 4

Prepping Time: 15 minutes

Cook Time: 25 minutes

Difficulty: Easy

Ingredients:

- 1 cup quinoa, rinsed and drained
- 2 cups vegetable broth
- 1 can (15 oz) black beans, drained and rinsed
- 1 cup corn kernels (fresh or frozen)

- 1 red bell pepper, diced
- 1 avocado, sliced
- 2 green onions, chopped
- 1/4 cup fresh cilantro, chopped
- 2 tablespoons lime juice
- 1 tablespoon olive oil
- Salt and pepper to taste

Step-by-Step Preparation:

- In a medium saucepan, combine quinoa and vegetable broth. Bring to a boil, then reduce heat and simmer for 15-20 minutes, or until quinoa is tender and liquid is absorbed.
- While cooking quinoa, combine black beans, corn, and red bell pepper in a large mixing bowl.
- Once quinoa is done, fluff it with a fork and allow it to cool slightly. Add it to the bean mixture.
- Drizzle with olive oil and lime juice, then toss to combine.
- Season with salt and pepper to taste.
- Divide the mixture among serving bowls. Top each with avocado slices, green onions, and fresh cilantro.

Nutritional Facts (Per serving):

- Calories: 320
- Protein: 12g
- Carbohydrates: 52g
- Dietary Fiber: 11g
- Fats: 9g
- Saturated Fat: 1.5g
- Sodium: 310mg

The Quinoa and Black Bean Bowl is a beacon of nutritional excellence in "Lunches for Lively Hearts". Venturing away from beef stir fry, this dish underscores the endless possibilities of plant-based ingredients, creating a harmony of tastes that resonates with wellness. As you explore the myriad offerings of this chapter, let each recipe serve as a testament to the beauty of health-conscious dining, ensuring that every lunch not only satisfies hunger but also kindles the heart's vitality. Embrace the journey of flavors and find joy in each nourishing bite.

Recipe 28: Tomato & Basil Zoodles

Savor the freshness of summer gardens with the Tomato & Basil Zoodles, a delightful play on traditional pasta. Eschewing beef stir fry and embracing the lightness of spiralized zucchini, this dish emerges as a standout in "Lunches for Lively Hearts". With ripe tomatoes and aromatic basil infusing their essence, this dish promises a culinary experience that's both refreshing and heart-healthy.

Servings: 4

Prepping Time: 10 minutes

Cook Time: 10 minutes

Difficulty: Easy

Ingredients:

- 4 medium zucchinis, spiralized into noodles
- 2 cups cherry tomatoes, halved
- 2 garlic cloves, minced
- 1/4 cup fresh basil, chopped

- 2 tablespoons extra virgin olive oil
- 1 teaspoon red pepper flakes (optional)
- Salt and pepper to taste
- Grated parmesan or crumbled feta for garnish (optional)

Step-by-Step Preparation:

- In a large pan, heat the olive oil over medium heat. Add minced garlic and red pepper flakes (if using) and sauté for a minute.
- Add the cherry tomatoes to the pan and cook for 5-7 minutes until they soften.
- Toss in the spiralized zucchini noodles, ensuring they're well combined with the tomatoes.
- Cook for another 2-3 minutes or until the zoodles are tender but still retain some crunch.
- Season with salt and pepper to taste.
- Remove from heat and stir in fresh chopped basil.
- Serve in bowls, garnished with your choice of cheese if desired.

Nutritional Facts (Per serving):

- Calories: 110
- Protein: 3g
- Carbohydrates: 11g
- Dietary Fiber: 3g
- Fats: 7g
- Saturated Fat: 1g
- Sodium: 20mg

Tomato & Basil Zoodles is a beautiful dance of simplicity and flavor, holding its own in "Lunches for Lively Hearts". By choosing zoodles over traditional pasta, you reduce carbs and embrace a delightful, crunchy texture. As you diverge from beef stir fry, remember that lunches hold boundless possibilities, each dish telling its own tale of nourishment and joy. Embark on this heart-healthy culinary journey, discovering dishes that caress the palate and nurture the heart with every flavorful bite.

Recipe 29: Spiced Sweet Potato & Lentil Salad

Savor the harmonious blend of earthy and zesty in the Spiced Sweet Potato & Lentil Salad, which champions wholesome ingredients in every bite. Although a divergence from beef stir fry, this salad holds its own in "Lunches for Lively Hearts". Melding the sweetness of roasted sweet potatoes with the heartiness of lentils and a sprinkle of spices, it's an ensemble that sings of nutrition and tantalizing flavors.

Servings: 4

Prepping Time: 20 minutes

Cook Time: 30 minutes

Difficulty: Medium

Ingredients:

- 2 medium sweet potatoes, diced
- 1 cup dried green lentils, rinsed and drained
- 4 cups vegetable broth
- 1 teaspoon ground cumin

- 1/2 teaspoon smoked paprika
- 2 tablespoons olive oil
- 1/4 cup fresh cilantro, chopped
- 2 tablespoons lemon juice
- Salt and pepper to taste
- Mixed greens for serving base

Step-by-Step Preparation:

- Preheat the oven to 425°F (220°C).
- Toss the diced sweet potatoes in a bowl with a tablespoon of olive oil, cumin, smoked paprika, salt, and pepper.
- Spread the seasoned sweet potatoes on a baking sheet and roast for 25-30 minutes until tender and slightly caramelized.
- Meanwhile, bring the vegetable broth to a boil in a medium saucepan. Add the lentils and simmer until tender, about 20 minutes. Drain any excess liquid.
- In a large bowl, combine the roasted sweet potatoes and cooked lentils.
- Drizzle with the remaining olive oil and lemon juice. Toss to combine.
- Serve atop mixed greens and garnish with fresh chopped cilantro.

Nutritional Facts (Per serving):

- Calories: 320
- Protein: 14g
- Carbohydrates: 55g
- Dietary Fiber: 16g
- Fats: 7g
- Saturated Fat: 1g
- Sodium: 220mg

The Spiced Sweet Potato & Lentil Salad offers a delicious alternative in "Lunches for Lively Hearts", pushing boundaries beyond beef stir fry. As you savor the richness of sweet potatoes and the wholesome goodness of lentils, let it be a testament to the beauty of plant-based meals. This salad not only tantalizes the taste buds but also promises heart-healthy nourishment with every bite. As you navigate this chapter, may each recipe remind you that a lively heart thrives on the flavors of diverse, nutritious ingredients woven together in delightful culinary tapestries?

Recipe 30: Tofu & Vegetable Stir-Fry

Embrace the delicate interplay of flavors and textures with the Tofu and vegetable Stir-Fry, which effortlessly marries health with gourmet appeal. Nestled within "Lunches for Lively Hearts", this recipe offers an exciting deviation from traditional beef stir fry. The silken touch of Tofu and the colorful array of crisp-tender vegetables bathed in a savory sauce is both a feast for the eyes and a treat for the palate.

Servings: 4

Prepping Time: 15 minutes

Cook Time: 20 minutes

Difficulty: Medium

Ingredients:

- 1 block of firm Tofu, cubed
- 2 cups broccoli florets
- 1 red bell pepper, sliced
- 1 carrot, julienned

- ❖ 2 green onions, chopped
- ❖ 3 tablespoons soy sauce (low sodium)
- ❖ 2 tablespoons sesame oil
- ❖ 1 tablespoon ginger, minced
- ❖ 2 garlic cloves, minced
- ❖ 1 tablespoon olive oil
- ❖ 1 teaspoon chili flakes (optional)
- ❖ Sesame seeds for garnish

Step-by-Step Preparation:

- ✓ Heat the olive oil over medium-high heat in a large pan or wok. Add the tofu cubes and stir-fry until golden brown on all sides. Remove and set aside.
- ✓ In the same pan, add the minced garlic and ginger and sauté briefly until aromatic.
- ✓ Introduce the broccoli, red bell pepper, and carrot to the pan. Stir-fry for 5-7 minutes or until vegetables are tender yet retain some crunch.
- ✓ Add the Tofu back into the pan, followed by the soy sauce, sesame oil, and chili flakes (if using). Mix well to ensure all ingredients are coated in the sauce.
- ✓ Cook for another 2-3 minutes, allowing flavors to meld.
- ✓ Garnish with chopped green onions and a sprinkle of sesame seeds before serving.

Nutritional Facts (Per serving):

- ❖ Calories: 210
- ❖ Protein: 12g
- ❖ Carbohydrates: 15g
- ❖ Dietary Fiber: 4g
- ❖ Fats: 12g
- ❖ Saturated Fat: 2g
- ❖ Sodium: 450mg

The Tofu and vegetable Stir-Fry encapsulates the culinary art of blending simple ingredients into a harmonious whole, making it a star in "Lunches for Lively Hearts". While distinct from the classic beef stir fry, it showcases how diverse ingredients can craft a heart-healthy and flavor-packed meal. Let this dish be a gentle reminder that lunches can be both nutritionally rich and gastronomically satisfying.

Chapter 04: Guilt-Free Afternoon Nibbles

Recipe 31: Nut & Seed Trail Mix

Venture into the delightful realm of crunchy, energy-boosting snacks with the Nut & Seed Trail Mix. As we navigate "Guilt-Free Afternoon Nibbles", it becomes evident that an afternoon pick-me-up doesn't have to be heavy like beef stir fry. This mix is a testament to the power of combining nutrient-dense ingredients, delivering a burst of energy and a symphony of flavors in every handful.

Servings: 10

Prepping Time: 10 minutes

Cook Time: 0 minutes (No cooking required)

Difficulty: Easy

Ingredients:

- 1 cup raw almonds

- ❖ 1/2 cup pumpkin seeds (pepitas)
- ❖ 1/2 cup sunflower seeds
- ❖ 1/2 cup dried cranberries
- ❖ 1/4 cup unsweetened coconut flakes
- ❖ 1/4 cup dark chocolate chips
- ❖ 1/4 cup raisins
- ❖ A pinch of sea salt

Step-by-Step Preparation:

- ✓ Combine almonds, pumpkin seeds, sunflower seeds, dried cranberries, and coconut flakes in a large mixing bowl.
- ✓ Add in the dark chocolate chips and raisins.
- ✓ Sprinkle a pinch of sea salt over the mixture and toss well to ensure even distribution of ingredients.
- ✓ Store the trail mix in an airtight container at room temperature. It remains fresh for up to 2 weeks.

Nutritional Facts (Per serving):

- ❖ Calories: 210
- ❖ Protein: 6g
- ❖ Carbohydrates: 18g
- ❖ Dietary Fiber: 4g
- ❖ Fats: 14g
- ❖ Saturated Fat: 3g
- ❖ Sodium: 20mg

The Nut & Seed Trail Mix is an ode to the joys of guilt-free snacking, shining brightly in "Guilt-Free Afternoon Nibbles". Moving beyond the heartiness of beef stir fry, this delightful concoction celebrates the simplicity and richness of nature's bounty. As you nibble away those afternoon hunger pangs, let this mix be a beacon of healthful indulgence. Dive deeper into this chapter and discover an array of snacks that gratify cravings and nourish the soul. Here's to snacking smartly, savoring every crunch and relishing the myriad flavors that afternoon delights can offer.

Recipe 32: Kale & Sea Salt Chips

Indulge in the crisped perfection of Kale and sea Salt Chips, a snack that combines the robust goodness of leafy greens with a touch of gourmet flair. Positioned within "Guilt-Free Afternoon Nibbles", this snack challenges traditional indulgences like beef stir fry, offering a lighter yet equally tantalizing choice. Each crisp carries the health benefits of Kale, making it a delightful alternative to commercial chips.

Servings: 4

Prepping Time: 10 minutes

Cook Time: 15 minutes

Difficulty: Easy

Ingredients:

- 1 large bunch of Kale, washed and dried
- 2 tablespoons olive oil
- 1/2 teaspoon of acceptable sea salt
- 1/4 teaspoon black pepper (optional)

Step-by-Step Preparation:

- ✓ Preheat the oven to 300°F (150°C).
- ✓ Remove the Kale leaves from the thick stems and tear them into chip-sized pieces.
- ✓ Toss the Kale with olive oil in a large bowl, ensuring each piece is lightly coated.
- ✓ Spread the Kale in a single layer on a baking sheet.
- ✓ Sprinkle with sea salt and black pepper (if using).
- ✓ Bake for 10-15 minutes or until the edges of the Kale are browned but not burnt.
- ✓ Allow chips to cool on the baking sheet for a few minutes before serving.

Nutritional Facts (Per serving):

- ❖ Calories: 70
- ❖ Protein: 2g
- ❖ Carbohydrates: 6g
- ❖ Dietary Fiber: 1g
- ❖ Fats: 5g
- ❖ Saturated Fat: 0.5g
- ❖ Sodium: 300mg

The Kale & Sea Salt Chips offer a new definition of snacking elegance in "Guilt-Free Afternoon Nibbles". Transitioning away from meaty indulgences like beef stir fry, this snack embraces the world of greens in its crispest form. As the afternoon sun dips and cravings beckon, let these chips be your go-to for a satisfying crunch, all while championing health and well-being. Continue exploring this chapter to unearth more such gems, each snack promising a blend of taste, health, and pure snacking pleasure. Remember, every nibble counts, and the right choices can turn simple munching moments into holistic experiences.

Recipe 33: Fresh Veggie Sticks with Guacamole

Dive into a vibrant world of crunch and zest with Fresh Veggie Sticks paired with a lusciously creamy Guacamole. As we navigate "Guilt-Free Afternoon Nibbles", this delightful snack provides a refreshing pause from the richness of dishes like beef stir fry. Celebrating the raw goodness of vegetables and the heart-healthy fats of avocados, this combo promises to be your ideal companion for light afternoon snacking.

Servings: 4

Prepping Time: 15 minutes

Cook Time: 0 minutes (No cooking required)

Difficulty: Easy

Ingredients:

- 2 ripe avocados, pitted and scooped out
- 1 small red onion, finely diced
- 1 tomato, finely chopped

- ❖ 1 jalapeño, seeds removed and minced (optional)
- ❖ 2 tablespoons fresh cilantro, chopped
- ❖ 1 lime, juiced
- ❖ Salt and pepper to taste
- ❖ Assorted fresh veggie sticks (carrots, bell peppers, cucumbers, celery)

Step-by-Step Preparation:

- ✓ Mash the avocados to your desired consistency in a mixing bowl using a fork.
- ✓ Add red onion, tomato, jalapeño (if using), and cilantro. Mix well.
- ✓ Squeeze in the lime juice and season with salt and pepper. Stir until well combined.
- ✓ Serve the guacamole immediately, accompanied by freshly sliced veggie sticks.

Nutritional Facts (Per serving):

- ❖ Calories: 190
- ❖ Protein: 3g
- ❖ Carbohydrates: 12g
- ❖ Dietary Fiber: 8g
- ❖ Fats: 16g
- ❖ Saturated Fat: 2g
- ❖ Sodium: 50mg

The Fresh Veggie Sticks with Guacamole capture the spirit of "Guilt-Free Afternoon Nibbles", championing the sheer joy of raw, vibrant ingredients. Distancing from heartier options like beef stir fry, this snack invites you to experience the purity and freshness of nature's bounty. Let it serve as a reminder that the simplest of ingredients, combined thoughtfully, can create culinary delights that satiate and invigorate. As you continue your foray into guilt-free nibbling, may each snack evoke a sense of joy, health, and boundless culinary creativity? Cheers to mindful munching.

Recipe 34: Almond Joy Energy Bites

Embark on a delightful culinary journey with the Almond Joy Energy Bites, where decadence meets nutrition. As we traverse "Guilt-Free Afternoon Nibbles", these bites introduce a sweet twist distinct from savory dishes like beef stir fry. Crafted with almonds, coconut, and a hint of chocolate, these morsels are designed to provide an instant energy boost while satisfying sweet cravings most healthily.

Servings: 12 bites

Prepping Time: 10 minutes

Cook Time: 0 minutes (No cooking required)

Difficulty: Easy

Ingredients:

- 1 cup raw almonds
- 1/2 cup shredded coconut, unsweetened
- 1/4 cup dark chocolate chips
- 8 medjool dates, pitted

- ❖ 1 tablespoon chia seeds
- ❖ 1 teaspoon vanilla extract
- ❖ A pinch of sea salt

Step-by-Step Preparation:

- ✓ Combine the almonds, shredded coconut, dates, chia seeds, vanilla extract, and sea salt in a food processor. Blend until the mixture is finely ground and starts to clump together.
- ✓ Add dark chocolate chips and pulse a few times to incorporate them into the mix.
- ✓ Using your hands, shape the mixture into bite-sized balls.
- ✓ Store the energy bites in an airtight container in the refrigerator for at least an hour before enjoying.

Nutritional Facts (Per serving):

- ❖ Calories: 110
- ❖ Protein: 3g
- ❖ Carbohydrates: 12g
- ❖ Dietary Fiber: 3g
- ❖ Fats: 7g
- ❖ Saturated Fat: 2g
- ❖ Sodium: 20mg

Almond Joy Energy Bites, showcased in "Guilt-Free Afternoon Nibbles", beckon with the promise of guilt-free indulgence. Moving away from the savory richness of beef stir fry, these bites emphasize the joys of sweet nibbles without compromising on health. Each bite melds nutty, coconutty, and chocolaty flavors into a symphony, proving that healthful snacks can be joyous. As you explore the breadth of this chapter, let every recipe be a testament to the art of combining taste with nourishment. Revel in the journey of snacking, where each bite not only satisfies the palate but also reenergizes the spirit. Here's to delightful afternoons filled with flavor and zest.

Recipe 35: Garlic & Herb Popcorn

Rediscover an all-time favorite snack with a gourmet twist in the Garlic and herb Popcorn. As you journey through "Guilt-Free Afternoon Nibbles", this popcorn stands apart from heartier dishes like beef stir fry. Elevated with aromatic garlic and a medley of herbs, this delightful snack transforms traditional popcorn into a wholesome and tantalizing, flavor-packed treat.

Servings: 4

Prepping Time: 5 minutes

Cook Time: 10 minutes

Difficulty: Easy

Ingredients:

- 1/2 cup popcorn kernels
- 3 tablespoons coconut oil or clarified butter
- 2 garlic cloves, finely minced
- 1 teaspoon dried rosemary
- 1 teaspoon dried thyme

- ❖ Salt to taste

Step-by-Step Preparation:

- ✓ Heat 2 tablespoons of coconut oil or clarified butter in a large pot over medium heat. Add the popcorn kernels.
- ✓ Cover the pot and shake occasionally to ensure even popping and prevent burning.
- ✓ Once the popping slows down, please remove it from the heat and let it sit for a minute.
- ✓ In a separate small pan, heat the remaining oil or butter. Add minced garlic, rosemary, and thyme, sautéing briefly until aromatic.
- ✓ Drizzle the garlic and herb-infused oil over the popped popcorn.
- ✓ Toss well to coat evenly and season with salt.

Nutritional Facts (Per serving):

- ❖ Calories: 140
- ❖ Protein: 2g
- ❖ Carbohydrates: 15g
- ❖ Dietary Fiber: 3g
- ❖ Fats: 8g
- ❖ Saturated Fat: 6g
- ❖ Sodium: 150mg

The Garlic and herb Popcorn is a nod to the beauty of simple yet flavorful snacking, proudly positioned in "Guilt-Free Afternoon Nibbles". Venturing beyond the realms of beef stir fry, this popcorn reminds us that the essence of a perfect snack lies in its capacity to marry health with flavor. As the aroma of garlic and herbs fills your space, let it be a testament to the endless possibilities that afternoon snacking can offer. Dive deeper into this chapter, letting each recipe inspire you to reimagine the boundaries of flavor, all while keeping health at the forefront. Here's to afternoons that surprise, delight, and nourish.

Recipe 36: Cholesterol-Free Chocolate Mousse

Indulge in the velvety embrace of the Cholesterol-Free Chocolate Mousse, a dessert that bridges the gap between luxury and well-being. Featured in "Guilt-Free Afternoon Nibbles", this mousse contrasts meaty dishes like beef stir fry. Crafted without traditional dairy, this dessert offers a rich, chocolaty experience that satiates the most discerning sweet tooth while ensuring heart health.

Servings: 4

Prepping Time: 10 minutes

Cook Time: 2 hours (chilling time)

Difficulty: Easy

Ingredients:

- 1 ripe avocado, peeled and pitted
- 1/4 cup unsweetened cocoa powder
- 1/4 cup maple syrup or agave nectar
- 1 teaspoon vanilla extract

- ❖ A pinch of sea salt
- ❖ Fresh berries for garnish (optional)

Step-by-Step Preparation:

- ✓ Combine the ripe avocado, cocoa powder, maple syrup, vanilla extract, and sea salt in a blender or food processor.
- ✓ Blend until the mixture is smooth and creamy, ensuring no avocado lumps remain.
- ✓ Taste and adjust sweetness, if necessary.
- ✓ Transfer the mousse to serving dishes and refrigerate for at least 2 hours to allow it to set.
- ✓ Before serving, garnish with fresh berries if desired.

Nutritional Facts (Per serving):

- ❖ Calories: 180
- ❖ Protein: 2g
- ❖ Carbohydrates: 25g
- ❖ Dietary Fiber: 6g
- ❖ Fats: 10g
- ❖ Saturated Fat: 1.5g
- ❖ Sodium: 30mg
- ❖ Cholesterol: 0mg

The Cholesterol-Free Chocolate Mousse, highlighted in "Guilt-Free Afternoon Nibbles", is a testament to the joy of reimagining dessert. As you step away from savory options like beef stir fry, this mousse invites you to savor the depth of cacao, harmonized beautifully with the creaminess of avocado. Beyond its decadent taste, the dessert's health benefits shine through, making every spoonful a celebration of balance and indulgence. Explore more in this chapter, allowing each recipe to redefine the parameters of afternoon snacking. In the dance between health and flavor, let's choreograph moments that linger, both on the palate and in memory. Cheers to wholesome indulgence.

Recipe 37: Spiced Roasted Chickpeas

Satisfy your crunch cravings with the Spiced Roasted Chickpeas, a snack that harmoniously merges health and flavor. As we delve into "Guilt-Free Afternoon Nibbles", these chickpeas offer a vibrant departure from dishes like beef stir fry. Roasted to perfection and adorned with an ensemble of spices, these chickpeas are set to be the star of your afternoon snacking, pairing protein richness with irresistible zest.

Servings: 4

Prepping Time: 10 minutes

Cook Time: 30 minutes

Difficulty: Easy

Ingredients:

- 1 can (15 oz) chickpeas, drained and rinsed
- 2 tablespoons olive oil
- 1 teaspoon ground cumin
- 1/2 teaspoon chili powder

- ❖ 1/4 teaspoon ground turmeric
- ❖ Salt to taste
- ❖ A dash of cayenne pepper (optional)

Step-by-Step Preparation:

- ✓ Preheat your oven to 425°F (220°C).
- ✓ Ensure the chickpeas are well-drained, and then pat them dry with a paper towel.
- ✓ In a mixing bowl, coat the chickpeas with olive oil, cumin, chili powder, turmeric, salt, and cayenne (if using).
- ✓ Spread them out evenly on a baking sheet.
- ✓ Roast in the preheated oven for 25-30 minutes, shaking the pan occasionally to ensure they roast evenly. They should be crispy and golden brown when done.
- ✓ Remove from the oven and allow them to cool before serving.

Nutritional Facts (Per serving):

- ❖ Calories: 155
- ❖ Protein: 6g
- ❖ Carbohydrates: 19g
- ❖ Dietary Fiber: 6g
- ❖ Fats: 7g
- ❖ Saturated Fat: 1g
- ❖ Sodium: 290mg

Spiced Roasted Chickpeas, brilliantly showcased in "Guilt-Free Afternoon Nibbles", exemplify the joy of transforming simple legumes into snack-time superstars. Veering away from traditional meaty delights like beef stir fry, this snack champions the essence of wholesome ingredients turned delightful. As you crunch through these chickpeas, let their flavors and nutrition remind you of the boundless possibilities in mindful snacking.

Recipe 38: Olive & Tomato Bruschetta

Experience the Mediterranean allure with the Olive and tomato Bruschetta, a delightful assembly of vibrant ingredients on toasted bread. As you meander through "Guilt-Free Afternoon Nibbles", this bruschetta offers a refreshing contrast to heavier dishes like beef stir fry. With the mingling of succulent tomatoes, zesty olives, and aromatic herbs, this classic Italian appetizer is a symphony of flavors, sure to rejuvenate any afternoon.

Servings: 4

Prepping Time: 10 minutes

Cook Time: 5 minutes

Difficulty: Easy

Ingredients:

- 4 slices of whole-grain baguette
- 1 cup cherry tomatoes, halved
- 1/2 cup pitted Kalamata olives, chopped
- 2 cloves garlic, minced

- ❖ 2 tablespoons fresh basil, chopped
- ❖ 1 tablespoon olive oil
- ❖ Salt and pepper to taste
- ❖ Grated Parmesan cheese (optional)

Step-by-Step Preparation:

- ✓ Preheat your oven to 400°F (200°C).
- ✓ Lightly brush the baguette slices with olive oil and toast them in the oven until golden brown.
- ✓ Combine cherry tomatoes, olives, garlic, and basil in a mixing bowl.
- ✓ Drizzle with olive oil, season with salt and pepper, and gently toss it.
- ✓ Top each toasted slice with the tomato and olive mixture.
- ✓ Garnish with grated Parmesan cheese if desired, and serve immediately.

Nutritional Facts (Per serving):

- ❖ Calories: 135
- ❖ Protein: 4g
- ❖ Carbohydrates: 18g
- ❖ Dietary Fiber: 3g
- ❖ Fats: 6g
- ❖ Saturated Fat: 1g
- ❖ Sodium: 290mg

The Olive & Tomato Bruschetta, highlighted in "Guilt-Free Afternoon Nibbles, " brings the promise of simplistic elegance in snacking. Steering clear of heartier alternatives like beef stir fry, this dish epitomizes how minimal ingredients can craft a mosaic of flavors. As the crunch of the toasted bread marries the freshness of tomatoes and olives, may this snack evoke sun-kissed Mediterranean afternoons? Navigate further into this chapter and revel in the art of crafting snacks that are as delightful to the senses as they nourish the body. To leisurely afternoons that are punctuated with gourmet experiences, salad.

Recipe 39: Raspberry Almond Bliss Balls

Whisk your taste buds away to a world of sweet serenity with Raspberry Almond Bliss Balls. Unveiling their charm in "Guilt-Free Afternoon Nibbles", these bliss balls present a delightful detour from savory dishes like beef stir fry. Infused with the tang of raspberries and the richness of almonds, these little treats promise to satiate your sweet cravings while being packed with natural goodness.

Servings: 12 balls

Prepping Time: 15 minutes

Cook Time: 0 minutes (No cooking required)

Difficulty: Easy

Ingredients:

- 1 cup almonds
- 1/2 cup dried raspberries
- 8 medjool dates, pitted
- 1 tablespoon chia seeds

- ❖ 2 tablespoons shredded coconut
- ❖ 1 teaspoon vanilla extract

Step-by-Step Preparation:

- ✓ Combine almonds, dried raspberries, dates, chia seeds, and vanilla extract in a food processor.
- ✓ Process until the mixture comes together and forms a sticky dough-like consistency.
- ✓ Scoop out spoonfuls of the mixture and shape them into balls using your hands.
- ✓ Roll each ball in shredded coconut for an added layer of texture and flavor.
- ✓ Store in an airtight container in the refrigerator for at least an hour before enjoying.

Nutritional Facts (Per serving):

- ❖ Calories: 110
- ❖ Protein: 3g
- ❖ Carbohydrates: 14g
- ❖ Dietary Fiber: 4g
- ❖ Fats: 6g
- ❖ Saturated Fat: 1g
- ❖ Sodium: 5mg

The Raspberry Almond Bliss Balls, a gem in "Guilt-Free Afternoon Nibbles", showcase how indulgence can beautifully intertwine with health. Moving away from the savory depths of beef stir fry, these bliss balls open the doors to a haven of natural sweetness and texture. Every bite, with its burst of raspberry tang and almond crunch, is a testament to the sheer pleasure of guilt-free snacking. As you continue your gastronomic journey through this chapter, let each nibble remind you of the limitless potential of natural ingredients. Here's to afternoons brimming with flavor, joy, and a touch of bliss.

Recipe 40: Oven-Baked Sweet Potato Fries

They are introducing the Oven-Baked Sweet Potato Fries, a vibrant twist on a classic favorite that promises taste and nutrition. In "Guilt-Free Afternoon Nibbles", while beef stir fry commands a savory spotlight, these fries shine with their natural sweetness and caramelized edges. Healthier than their traditional counterparts, these golden batons invite you to indulge without guilt.

Servings: 4

Prepping Time: 10 minutes

Cook Time: 25-30 minutes

Difficulty: Easy

Ingredients:

- 2 large sweet potatoes, peeled and cut into wedges
- 2 tablespoons olive oil
- 1 teaspoon smoked paprika
- Salt and pepper to taste

- ❖ Fresh parsley, chopped (for garnish)

Step-by-Step Preparation:

- ✓ Preheat your oven to 425°F (220°C).
- ✓ Toss sweet potato wedges with olive oil, smoked paprika, salt, and pepper in a large bowl.
- ✓ Spread the coated wedges on a baking sheet in a single layer, ensuring they don't overlap.
- ✓ Bake for 25-30 minutes, flipping halfway, until the fries are golden and crisp on the edges.
- ✓ Once out of the oven, sprinkle with chopped parsley and serve immediately.

Nutritional Facts (Per serving):

- ❖ Calories: 155
- ❖ Protein: 2g
- ❖ Carbohydrates: 29g
- ❖ Dietary Fiber: 4g
- ❖ Fats: 5g
- ❖ Saturated Fat: 0.7g
- ❖ Sodium: 80mg

The Oven-Baked Sweet Potato Fries, a star in "Guilt-Free Afternoon Nibbles", are a testament to the magic that simple ingredients can create. Venturing beyond the hearty realm of beef stir fry, these fries redefine the concept of afternoon snacking with their delightful blend of sweetness and spice. Every crunch encapsulates the joys of guilt-free indulgence, reminding us that healthy choices can be incredibly delicious. Dive deeper into this chapter, allowing the curated recipes to uplift your snacking game. Every nibble, from savory to sweet, echoes a commitment to flavor and well-being.

Chapter 05: Delicious Dinners Low in Cholesterol

Recipe 41: Lemon Herb Grilled Salmon

Dive into a culinary masterpiece with the Lemon Herb Grilled Salmon, an entrée that marries the richness of the sea with the zest of citrus and aromatic herbs. As we navigate "Delicious Dinners Low in Cholesterol", this salmon dish emerges as a delightful alternative to the familiar flavors of beef stir fry. Bursting with omega-3s and effortlessly seasoned, this entrée is both a feast for the eyes and a boon for the heart.

Servings: 4

Prepping Time: 15 minutes

Cook Time: 15 minutes

Difficulty: Moderate

Ingredients:

- 4 salmon fillets
- 2 lemons, zested and juiced
- 2 tablespoons olive oil
- 2 cloves garlic, minced
- 1 tablespoon fresh dill, chopped
- 1 tablespoon fresh parsley, chopped
- Salt and pepper to taste

Step-by-Step Preparation:

- ✓ Combine lemon zest, lemon juice, olive oil, garlic, dill, parsley, salt, and pepper in a mixing bowl. Whisk well to form a marinade.
- ✓ Place the salmon fillets in a shallow dish and pour the marinade over them, ensuring they're well-coated.
- ✓ Let the salmon marinate for at least 30 minutes in the refrigerator.
- ✓ Preheat the grill to medium-high heat.
- ✓ Place the salmon fillets on the grill and cook for 6-7 minutes on each side or until the fish flakes easily with a fork.
- ✓ Remove from the grill and serve immediately, garnished with extra herbs and lemon slices if desired.

Nutritional Facts (Per serving):

- Calories: 275
- Protein: 31g
- Carbohydrates: 3g
- Dietary Fiber: 1g
- Fats: 16g
- Saturated Fat: 2.5g
- Sodium: 100mg
- Cholesterol: 70mg

The Lemon Herb Grilled Salmon, gracefully positioned in "Delicious Dinners Low in Cholesterol", is a testament to culinary excellence that embraces health without compromising taste. As you step away from the comfort of beef stir fry, this salmon dish exemplifies how quality ingredients and thoughtful seasoning can craft an unforgettable dining experience. Every bite is an ode to the richness of the sea, enhanced by the freshness of herbs and the zest of lemon.

Recipe 42: Whole Wheat Spaghetti with Fresh Tomato Sauce

As we journey through "Delicious Dinners Low in Cholesterol", this pasta dish offers a heartwarming, nutritious alternative to the familiar richness of beef stir fry. The wholesome goodness of whole wheat meets the vibrant freshness of tomatoes, culminating in a dish as nourishing as it is delightful.

Servings: 4

Prepping Time: 15 minutes

Cook Time: 20 minutes

Difficulty: Easy

Ingredients:

- 8 oz whole wheat spaghetti
- 4 ripe tomatoes, diced
- 2 cloves garlic, minced
- 2 tablespoons olive oil
- 1 teaspoon dried basil

- 1 teaspoon dried oregano
- Salt and pepper to taste
- Fresh basil leaves for garnish
- Grated Parmesan cheese (optional)

Step-by-Step Preparation:

- ✓ Cook the whole wheat spaghetti according to package instructions until al dente.
- ✓ In a saucepan, heat the olive oil over medium heat. Add the minced garlic and sauté until fragrant.
- ✓ Add the diced tomatoes, dried basil, oregano, salt, and pepper. Simmer for 15 minutes, allowing the flavors to meld.
- ✓ Once the spaghetti is cooked, drain and add it to the sauce, tossing to coat thoroughly.
- ✓ Serve immediately, garnished with fresh basil leaves and an optional sprinkle of grated Parmesan cheese.

Nutritional Facts (Per serving):

- Calories: 270
- Protein: 9g
- Carbohydrates: 47g
- Dietary Fiber: 7g
- Fats: 7g
- Saturated Fat: 1g
- Sodium: 90mg
- Cholesterol: 0mg

The Whole Wheat Spaghetti with Fresh Tomato Sauce, masterfully presented in "Delicious Dinners Low in Cholesterol", epitomizes the beauty of simple, wholesome dining. Stepping away from the heartiness of beef stir fry, this dish sings praises of nature's bounty, with each strand of pasta capturing the essence of fresh tomatoes. The merger of rustic Italian flavors with health-conscious choices showcases that mindful dining can be delectably satisfying. As you explore this chapter, let every recipe serve as testaments to culinary delights that not only tantalize the taste buds but also nurture the body. To evenings filled with gastronomic joy and heart-friendly choices, salute.

Recipe 43: Garlic-infused Olive Oil & Veggie Stir-Fry

Delve into the heart of a healthful culinary experience with this "Garlic-infused Olive Oil & Veggie Stir-Fry." Skillfully balancing the robust flavor of garlic with tender beef and vibrant vegetables, this dish promises a delectable dance of textures and tastes on your palate. As part of this recipe assures a dinner that is not just flavorsome but also remarkably low in cholesterol, making it a perfect pick for heart-conscious gourmets.

Servings: 4

Prepping Time: 15 minutes

Cook Time: 20 minutes

Difficulty: Moderate

Ingredients:

- 500g lean beef slices
- 3 tbsp garlic-infused olive oil
- 1 red bell pepper, julienned

- ❖ 1 yellow bell pepper, julienned
- ❖ 1 cup broccoli florets
- ❖ 1 carrot, thinly sliced
- ❖ 2 tbsp low-sodium soy sauce
- ❖ 1 tsp sesame seeds (optional)
- ❖ Salt and pepper, to taste

Step-by-Step Preparation:

- ✓ Heat the garlic-infused olive oil over medium heat in a large skillet or wok.
- ✓ Add the beef slices and cook until browned. Remove and set aside.
- ✓ Add bell peppers, broccoli, and carrot in the same skillet. Stir-fry for about 5-7 minutes or until vegetables are tender-crisp.
- ✓ Return the beef to the skillet and pour in the soy sauce. Stir well to combine.
- ✓ Season with salt and pepper, and sprinkle with sesame seeds if desired.
- ✓ Serve immediately with steamed rice or noodles.

Nutritional Facts: (Per serving)

- ❖ Calories: 320
- ❖ Cholesterol: 45mg
- ❖ Protein: 25g
- ❖ Carbohydrates: 12g
- ❖ Fiber: 3g
- ❖ Sugars: 5g
- ❖ Fat: 18g
- ❖ Sodium: 350mg

Ah, the simple joy of devouring a plate full of delectable stir-fry! While the tender beef offers a burst of protein, the garden-fresh veggies provide an essential dose of vitamins and fiber, making the dish both nourishing and delicious. The star, however, is the garlic-infused olive oil, lending the meal its aromatic richness without piling on the cholesterol. A delightful way to enjoy dinner, this dish showcases how healthy choices needn't compromise on flavor. As you continue through let this recipe be a testament to the wonders of heart-friendly yet palatable dinners.

Recipe 44: Oven-Roasted Herb Chicken

Savor the rich symphony of herbs and spices as they meld perfectly with tender chicken in this "Oven-Roasted Herb Chicken" recipe. It is a beautifully aromatic and golden-brown dish on the outside, yet moist and flavorful. While this sounds like a classic roast, our take is carefully crafted for ensuring that cholesterol remains in check while flavor is at its peak. The perfect blend of health and taste promises to elevate your dinner to a gourmet experience.

Servings: 4

Prepping Time: 20 minutes

Cook Time: 45 minutes

Difficulty: Moderate

Ingredients:

- ❖ 4 boneless, skinless chicken breasts
- ❖ 3 tbsp olive oil
- ❖ 2 tsp rosemary, finely chopped

- ❖ 2 tsp thyme, finely chopped
- ❖ 3 garlic cloves, minced
- ❖ 1 lemon, zested and juiced
- ❖ Salt and pepper, to taste

Step-by-Step Preparation:

- ✓ Preheat the oven to 375°F (190°C).
- ✓ Mix olive oil, rosemary, thyme, garlic, lemon zest, and juice in a bowl.
- ✓ Season the chicken breasts with salt and pepper.
- ✓ Brush each chicken breast with the herb mixture, ensuring it's well coated.
- ✓ Place the chicken on a roasting tray lined with parchment paper or foil.
- ✓ Roast in the oven for about 40-45 minutes or until the chicken is fully cooked and has a golden-brown exterior.
- ✓ Let it rest for 5 minutes before serving.

Nutritional Facts: (Per serving)

- ❖ Calories: 290
- ❖ Cholesterol: 85mg
- ❖ Protein: 30g
- ❖ Carbohydrates: 4g
- ❖ Fiber: 1g
- ❖ Sugars: 1g
- ❖ Fat: 16g
- ❖ Sodium: 250mg

Indulge in the elegance of a beautifully roasted chicken, where every bite brings forth the whispers of fragrant herbs and zesty lemon undertones. This Oven-Roasted Herb Chicken offers a feast for your senses and adheres to our commitment in crafting meals that are luxuriously tasty yet gentle on cholesterol levels. As you explore the rest of the chapter, may this dish be a delightful reminder that heart-healthy choices can be tantalizing to the taste buds? Dive into this culinary masterpiece and relish the sheer joy of wholesome dining.

Recipe 45: Stuffed Bell Peppers with Quinoa & Veggies

Delight in a harmonious blend of wholesome quinoa and vibrant vegetables, all snugly nestled inside a tender bell pepper in our "Stuffed Bell Peppers with Quinoa & Veggies" recipe. This dish is a celebration of flavors, colors, and textures, and while it strays from the beef stir fry theme of it upholds our commitment to offering dinners that are not just tantalizing but also exceptionally low in cholesterol. Dive into this culinary adventure where every bite is both nutritious and delicious.

Servings: 4

Prepping Time: 20 minutes

Cook Time: 30 minutes

Difficulty: Easy

Ingredients:

- ❖ 4 large bell peppers (varied colors)
- ❖ 1 cup cooked quinoa

- ❖ 1 cup diced zucchini
- ❖ 1 cup cherry tomatoes, halved
- ❖ 1/2 cup corn kernels
- ❖ 1/2 cup black beans, drained and rinsed
- ❖ 2 tbsp olive oil
- ❖ 1 tsp cumin
- ❖ Salt and pepper, to taste
- ❖ Fresh cilantro for garnish

Step-by-Step Preparation:

- ✓ Preheat the oven to 375°F (190°C).
- ✓ Cut the tops off the bell peppers and remove the seeds.
- ✓ Combine quinoa, zucchini, cherry tomatoes, corn, and black beans in a large bowl.
- ✓ Drizzle olive oil, sprinkle cumin, salt, and pepper, and mix well.
- ✓ Stuff each bell pepper with the quinoa and veggie mixture, pressing down gently.
- ✓ Place the stuffed bell peppers in a baking dish and cover with foil.
- ✓ Bake for 25-30 minutes or until peppers are tender.
- ✓ Garnish with fresh cilantro before serving.

Nutritional Facts: (Per serving)

- ❖ Calories: 220
- ❖ Cholesterol: 0mg
- ❖ Protein: 7g
- ❖ Carbohydrates: 35g
- ❖ Fiber: 7g
- ❖ Sugars: 6g
- ❖ Fat: 7g
- ❖ Sodium: 80mg

Embrace the magic of a meal that offers the coziness of home-cooked fare paired with the elegance of fine dining. The "Stuffed Bell Peppers with Quinoa & Veggies" is more than just a dish; it's an experience. Each pepper is a treasure trove of nutrients, flavors, and textures, promising satisfaction with every bite. As you journey through remember this culinary gem as a testament that low-cholesterol dinners can be as delectable as they are healthy. Here's to a dinner choice that beautifully marries health with indulgence.

Recipe 46: Grilled Eggplant & Zucchini Platter

Evoke the allure of alfresco dining with our "Grilled Eggplant & Zucchini Platter." While this dish diverges from the beef stir fry essence of it embodies the chapter's dedication to heart-healthy, low-cholesterol dinners. The smoky notes of the grilled vegetables, complemented by a light seasoning, make for an effortlessly elegant dish that's as delightful to the palate as beneficial to the heart.

Servings: 4

Prepping Time: 15 minutes

Cook Time: 20 minutes

Difficulty: Easy

Ingredients:

- 2 medium eggplants, sliced
- 2 medium zucchinis, sliced
- 3 tbsp olive oil
- 2 garlic cloves, minced

- ❖ Salt and pepper, to taste
- ❖ Fresh basil leaves for garnish
- ❖ Lemon wedges for serving

Step-by-Step Preparation:

- ✓ Preheat the grill to medium heat.
- ✓ In a bowl, mix olive oil and minced garlic.
- ✓ Brush each slice of eggplant and zucchini with the garlic-infused oil.
- ✓ Season with salt and pepper.
- ✓ Place the vegetable slices on the grill and cook for 3-4 minutes on each side or until grill marks appear and they are tender.
- ✓ Remove from grill and arrange on a platter.
- ✓ Garnish with fresh basil leaves and serve with lemon wedges.

Nutritional Facts: (Per serving)

- ❖ Calories: 130
- ❖ Cholesterol: 0mg
- ❖ Protein: 2g
- ❖ Carbohydrates: 12g
- ❖ Fiber: 5g
- ❖ Sugars: 7g
- ❖ Fat: 9g
- ❖ Sodium: 5mg

The "Grilled Eggplant & Zucchini Platter" is a testament to nature's bounty, highlighting simple, grilled vegetables' sheer beauty and flavor. It's a dish that pays homage to the Mediterranean coasts, capturing the essence of sun-kissed days and breezy evenings. As you journey through the pages of let this recipe be a gentle reminder that low-cholesterol dinners don't need to be complex to be captivating. Celebrate the beauty of simplicity, the joys of wholesome ingredients, and the pleasure of a heart-healthy meal, all plated in this delightful dish.

Recipe 47: Vegan Thai Green Curry

Transport your senses to the bustling streets of Thailand with our "Vegan Thai Green Curry." Although a departure from the beef stir fry theme dominant in this curry maintains our devotion to low-cholesterol dishes without compromising on authentic flavors. Infused with aromatic herbs and rich coconut milk, this vegan delight offers a burst of flavors, ensuring a gourmet experience in every spoonful.

Servings: 4

Prepping Time: 20 minutes

Cook Time: 30 minutes

Difficulty: Moderate

Ingredients:

- 2 cups mixed vegetables (bell peppers, zucchini, snap peas, etc.)
- 400ml can of coconut milk
- 3 tbsp Thai green curry paste
- 1 tbsp coconut oil

- 1 onion, finely sliced
- 2 garlic cloves, minced
- 1-inch ginger, grated
- Fresh basil leaves for garnish
- Salt, to taste

Step-by-Step Preparation:

- In a large pan, heat coconut oil over medium heat.
- Sauté onion, garlic, and ginger until the onion becomes translucent.
- Stir in the Thai green curry paste, ensuring the aromatics are well-coated.
- Pour in the coconut milk and bring the mixture to a gentle simmer.
- Add the mixed vegetables, season with salt, and let it cook for 20-25 minutes or until vegetables are tender.
- Adjust seasoning if necessary.
- Serve hot, garnished with fresh basil leaves.

Nutritional Facts: (Per serving)

- Calories: 240
- Cholesterol: 0mg
- Protein: 4g
- Carbohydrates: 20g
- Fiber: 4g
- Sugars: 5g
- Fat: 18g
- Sodium: 370mg

Embracing the vibrant flavors of Thailand our "Vegan Thai Green Curry" stands as a beacon of culinary excellence that's heart-friendly and palate-pleasing. With its luscious, creamy texture and a symphony of flavors, this dish promises a delightful escape from the ordinary. As you delve deeper into let this vegan masterpiece underscore that low-cholesterol dining can be an adventure filled with global flavors and memorable experiences. Here's to health, taste, and the unparalleled joy of exploring authentic cuisines.

Recipe 48: Heart-Friendly Ratatouille

Step into the rustic charm of French provincial cuisine with the "Heart-Friendly Ratatouille." A delightful deviation from the beef stir fry theme of this dish holds to our pledge of crafting delicious meals while keeping cholesterol in check. Composed of a medley of slow-cooked vegetables in a rich tomato sauce, this classic Mediterranean recipe is an ode to simple ingredients transforming into a symphony of flavors.

Servings: 4

Prepping Time: 25 minutes

Cook Time: 40 minutes

Difficulty: Easy

Ingredients:

- 2 zucchinis, sliced
- 2 eggplants, cubed
- 1 bell pepper, chopped
- 2 tomatoes, diced

- ❖ 1 onion, finely sliced
- ❖ 3 garlic cloves, minced
- ❖ 3 tbsp olive oil
- ❖ 1 tsp dried basil
- ❖ Salt and pepper, to taste
- ❖ Fresh parsley for garnish

Step-by-Step Preparation:

- ✓ In a large pot, heat olive oil over medium heat.
- ✓ Add onions and garlic, sautéing until translucent.
- ✓ Introduce bell peppers, followed by zucchinis and eggplants.
- ✓ Once slightly softened, mix in tomatoes.
- ✓ Season with dried basil, salt, and pepper.
- ✓ Reduce heat, cover, and let simmer for 30-35 minutes, stirring occasionally.
- ✓ Check the season and adjust if needed.
- ✓ Serve hot, garnished with freshly chopped parsley.

Nutritional Facts: (Per serving)

- ❖ Calories: 150
- ❖ Cholesterol: 0mg
- ❖ Protein: 3g
- ❖ Carbohydrates: 19g
- ❖ Fiber: 6g
- ❖ Sugars: 11g
- ❖ Fat: 9g
- ❖ Sodium: 20mg

Embarking on a gastronomic journey through the sun-drenched fields of France, our "Heart-Friendly Ratatouille" encapsulates the warmth of traditional home cooking with a heart-conscious twist. Every bite unveils layers of taste, a testament to the magic of slow-cooked veggies in harmonious unity. As you progress through this dish is a beautiful reminder that culinary traditions worldwide can be seamlessly adapted to fit a heart-healthy lifestyle. Relish this sumptuous dish, celebrating the richness of French cuisine and the joy of mindful eating.

Recipe 49: Barley & Vegetable Risotto

Infuse your dining experience with the wholesome goodness of "Barley & Vegetable Risotto." While veering away from the beef stir fry focus of this dish remains steadfast in its promise to offer dinners that are brimming with flavor while being considerate of cholesterol levels. With its nutty undertones, Barley pairs beautifully with vibrant vegetables to create a comforting and heart-friendly risotto.

Servings: 4

Prepping Time: 20 minutes

Cook Time: 45 minutes

Difficulty: Moderate

Ingredients:

- 1 cup pearl barley
- 2 cups mixed vegetables (zucchini, bell peppers, carrots)
- 1 onion, finely diced
- 3 garlic cloves, minced

- ❖ 4 cups low-sodium vegetable broth
- ❖ 2 tbsp olive oil
- ❖ 1/2 cup grated Parmesan cheese (optional)
- ❖ Salt and pepper, to taste
- ❖ Fresh parsley, chopped, for garnish

Step-by-Step Preparation:

- ✓ In a large saucepan, heat olive oil over medium flame.
- ✓ Sauté onions and garlic until translucent.
- ✓ Introduce the mixed vegetables and stir for a couple of minutes.
- ✓ Add in the Barley, ensuring each grain gets coated with the oil.
- ✓ Pour in the vegetable broth, one cup at a time, stirring constantly and allowing each addition to be absorbed before adding the next.
- ✓ Continue this process until the Barley is tender and creamy.
- ✓ Season with salt and pepper, and stir in the Parmesan cheese if desired.
- ✓ Garnish with freshly chopped parsley before serving.

Nutritional Facts: (Per serving)

- ❖ Calories: 280
- ❖ Cholesterol: 5mg (with cheese)
- ❖ Protein: 8g
- ❖ Carbohydrates: 50g
- ❖ Fiber: 10g
- ❖ Sugars: 4g
- ❖ Fat: 8g
- ❖ Sodium: 150mg

Dive into the comforting embrace of the "Barley & Vegetable Risotto," a dish that champions the fusion of rustic grains and fresh produce. This meal is a testament to the beauty of simple ingredients transforming into a gastronomic delight. As you navigate the pages of may this recipe illuminate the idea that low-cholesterol meals can be as heartwarming as they are heart-healthy? Indulge in this delightful risotto, celebrating the age-old love affair between grains and veggies, ideally suited for a cholesterol-conscious age.

Recipe 50: Lentil & Mushroom Stuffed Acorn Squash

Venture into a culinary experience that bridges comfort with sophistication in the "Lentil & Mushroom Stuffed Acorn Squash." While this dish diverges from the beef stir fry narrative of it retains our commitment to delivering sumptuous meals while mindful of cholesterol levels. The earthy undertones of lentils and mushrooms, cradled within the subtly sweet acorn squash, present a dish that's as nourishing as it is visually captivating.

Servings: 4

Prepping Time: 20 minutes

Cook Time: 50 minutes

Difficulty: Moderate

Ingredients:

- 2 acorn squashes, halved, and seeds removed
- 1 cup cooked green lentils
- 1 cup mushrooms, finely chopped

- ❖ 1 onion, finely diced
- ❖ 2 garlic cloves, minced
- ❖ 2 tbsp olive oil
- ❖ 1 tsp fresh thyme leaves
- ❖ Salt and pepper, to taste
- ❖ Fresh parsley, chopped, for garnish

Step-by-Step Preparation:

- ✓ Preheat oven to 375°F (190°C).
- ✓ Brush the inside of each acorn squash half with olive oil, season with salt, and place face-down on a baking tray. Bake for 35-40 minutes or until tender.
- ✓ In a pan, heat the remaining olive oil over medium heat. Add onions and garlic, sautéing until translucent.
- ✓ Incorporate the mushrooms and cook until they release their juices and become tender.
- ✓ Stir in the lentils, thyme, salt, and pepper, cooking for another 5 minutes.
- ✓ Remove the squashes from the oven and carefully fill each half with the lentil-mushroom mixture.
- ✓ Garnish with freshly chopped parsley before serving.

Nutritional Facts: (Per serving)

- ❖ Calories: 230
- ❖ Cholesterol: 0mg
- ❖ Protein: 9g
- ❖ Carbohydrates: 42g
- ❖ Fiber: 8g
- ❖ Sugars: 4g
- ❖ Fat: 5g
- ❖ Sodium: 50mg

Savor the elegance and simplicity of the "Lentil & Mushroom Stuffed Acorn Squash," a delightful fusion of nutrient-rich ingredients in a gourmet style. As you immerse yourself in culinary journey, let this dish stand as a beacon, emphasizing that meals with low cholesterol can seamlessly merge health and haute cuisine. Relish this harmonious blend of textures and flavors, affirming that heart-healthy choices can be delightful and distinguished.

Chapter 06: Light and Luscious

Recipe 51: Dark Chocolate Covered Almonds

Indulge in the timeless combination of rich dark chocolate and crunchy almonds with our "Dark Chocolate Covered Almonds." While a departure from the beef stir fry motif, this sumptuous treat aligns perfectly with theme of "Light and Luscious." Balancing the antioxidant-rich goodness of dark chocolate with the heart-healthy benefits of almonds, these delights offer indulgence and nutrition in every bite.

Servings: 6

Prepping Time: 10 minutes

Cook Time: 5 minutes

Difficulty: Easy

Ingredients:

- ❖ 1 cup raw almonds

- 200g high-quality dark chocolate (70% cocoa or above)
- 1/2 tsp sea salt (optional)
- 1 tsp coconut oil

Step-by-Step Preparation:

- Melt the dark chocolate and coconut oil in a heatproof bowl over a pot of simmering water, ensuring the bowl doesn't touch the water.
- Once the chocolate is smooth and fully melted, remove from heat.
- Toss in the almonds, ensuring each one is well-coated with the chocolate.
- Using a fork, remove each almond and place it on a parchment-lined tray, ensuring they don't touch.
- Sprinkle with sea salt if desired.
- Place the tray in the refrigerator for 30 minutes or until the chocolate hardens.
- Store in an airtight container.

Nutritional Facts: (Per serving)

- Calories: 180
- Cholesterol: 0mg
- Protein: 4g
- Carbohydrates: 12g
- Fiber: 3g
- Sugars: 7g
- Fat: 14g
- Sodium: 85mg (with added salt)

Satisfy your sweet cravings with the luxurious "Dark Chocolate Covered Almonds," a treat that pairs decadence with well-being. As you navigate the lighthearted and flavorful selections of let this recipe be a testament to the joy of indulging mindfully. Every bite delivers the dual pleasure of creamy chocolate and nutty crunch, reminding us that it's possible to treat ourselves without compromising health. So, the next time you yearn for indulgence, reach for these gems, knowing you're choosing pleasure and nutrition. Celebrate the art of guilt-free snacking.

Recipe 52: Greek Yogurt & Mixed Berry Parfait

Elevate your dessert experience with the refreshing "Greek Yogurt & Mixed Berry Parfait layers." A delightful deviation from the beef stir fry trend, this creation aligns seamlessly with emphasis on "Light and Luscious." The creaminess of the Greek yogurt, complemented by the natural sweetness of mixed berries and a hint of granola crunch, crafts a dessert that's as pleasing to the palate as it is beneficial for health.

Servings: 4

Prepping Time: 10 minutes

Cook Time: 0 minutes

Difficulty: Easy

Ingredients:

- 2 cups Greek yogurt
- 1 cup mixed berries (blueberries, strawberries, raspberries)
- 1/2 cup granola
- 2 tbsp honey or maple syrup

- ❖ 1 tsp vanilla extract
- ❖ Fresh mint leaves, for garnish

Step-by-Step Preparation:

- ✓ Mix the Greek yogurt with honey or maple syrup and vanilla extract in a bowl until smooth.
- ✓ Begin layering the parfait in individual glasses. Start with a spoonful of Greek yogurt at the base.
- ✓ Add a layer of mixed berries, followed by a sprinkle of granola.
- ✓ Repeat the layers until the glass are filled, finishing with a layer of berries on top.
- ✓ Garnish with a fresh mint leaf.
- ✓ Serve immediately or refrigerate for later use.

Nutritional Facts: (Per serving)

- ❖ Calories: 190
- ❖ Cholesterol: 5mg
- ❖ Protein: 11g
- ❖ Carbohydrates: 25g
- ❖ Fiber: 2g
- ❖ Sugars: 18g
- ❖ Fat: 4g
- ❖ Sodium: 40mg

Relish the symphony of textures and flavors in the "Greek Yogurt & Mixed Berry Parfait," a dessert that marries indulgence with nourishment. As you explore the culinary wonders of this creation stands as a testament to the fact that light and luscious can coexist harmoniously in a single dish. Perfect for breakfast, dessert, or a midday treat, this parfait celebrates the beauty of simple ingredients coming together in a dance of flavors. Dive into this delightful concoction, cherishing the balance of creamy, crunchy, and fruity in every spoonful, and savor the essence of mind indulgence.

Recipe 53: Peanut Butter & Celery Sticks

Revisit a childhood favorite with a delightful spin in "Peanut Butter & Celery Sticks." Straying from the beef stir fry narrative, this snack perfectly embodies "Light and Luscious" essence. The creamy, rich taste of peanut butter, when paired with the fresh crunch of celery, creates a snack that's heart-healthy and incredibly satisfying, making snacking fun and beneficial.

Servings: 4

Prepping Time: 10 minutes

Cook Time: 0 minutes

Difficulty: Easy

Ingredients:

- 8 celery stalks, washed and trimmed
- 1/2 cup natural peanut butter
- 1/4 cup raisins or dried cranberries (optional)
- A pinch of salt (if unsalted peanut butter is used)

Step-by-Step Preparation:

- ✓ Ensure the celery stalks are dry by patting them with a paper towel.
- ✓ Spread a generous amount of peanut butter into the groove of each celery stick.
- ✓ If desired, sprinkle raisins or dried cranberries on top for added sweetness and texture.
- ✓ Arrange the prepared sticks on a platter and serve.

Nutritional Facts: (Per serving)

- ❖ Calories: 140
- ❖ Cholesterol: 0mg
- ❖ Protein: 5g
- ❖ Carbohydrates: 10g
- ❖ Fiber: 3g
- ❖ Sugars: 5g (without added raisins or cranberries)
- ❖ Fat: 10g
- ❖ Sodium: 90mg

The humble pairing of "Peanut Butter and celery Sticks" is a beautiful reminder that simplicity often brings forth the most delightful flavors. As you journey through cherish this snack as evidence that light and lusciousness coexist harmoniously. Whether seeking a quick midday pick-me-up or a health-conscious after-dinner treat, this combination promises satisfaction in every crunchy bite. So, here's to relishing the joys of minimalism in snacking, where every ingredient shines and contributes to a wholesome experience. Cheers to smart snacking.

Recipe 54: Cinnamon Spiced Apple Slices

Embark on a sensory journey with the "Cinnamon Spiced Apple Slices." Moving away from the beef stir fry theme, this delightful snack encapsulates the essence of "Light and Luscious." The natural sweetness of apples, kissed with a sprinkle of warming cinnamon, crafts a snack that is as heartwarming as health-conscious. This combination not only tantalizes the taste buds but also evokes the coziness of a crisp autumn day.

Servings: 4

Prepping Time: 10 minutes

Cook Time: 0 minutes

Difficulty: Easy

Ingredients:

- 4 medium-sized apples, preferably crisp varieties like Honeycrisp or Fuji
- 2 tsp ground cinnamon
- 1 tsp honey or maple syrup (optional)

- ❖ Fresh mint leaves for garnish (optional)

Step-by-Step Preparation:

- ✓ Wash and core the apples.
- ✓ Slice the apples into thin rounds or wedges, as per preference.
- ✓ In a large mixing bowl, gently toss the apple slices with ground cinnamon, ensuring each slice is lightly coated.
- ✓ If desired, drizzle with honey or maple syrup for added sweetness.
- ✓ If desired, serve the spiced apple slices on a platter, garnished with fresh mint leaves.

Nutritional Facts: (Per serving)

- ❖ Calories: 95
- ❖ Cholesterol: 0mg
- ❖ Protein: 0.5g
- ❖ Carbohydrates: 25g
- ❖ Fiber: 4g
- ❖ Sugars: 19g (without added honey or syrup)
- ❖ Fat: 0.3g
- ❖ Sodium: 2mg

With every bite of the "Cinnamon Spiced Apple Slices," you're transported to an orchard in golden sunlight, where nature's bounty meets culinary simplicity. As you delve deeper into let this recipe serve as a testament to the elegance of minimalism in snacking. Satisfying, refreshing, and brimming with flavor, these apple slices are a perfect testament to the chapter's commitment to light and luscious delights. So, as you savor each spiced slice, please take a moment to appreciate the beauty of natural flavors and the warmth they bring to our plates and palates.

Recipe 55: Light Popcorn with Nutritional Yeast

Unwind with a bowl of "Light Popcorn with Nutritional Yeast," a modern twist on a timeless snacking classic. Veering from the beef stir fry trajectory, this snack perfectly embodies the ethos of "Light and Luscious" theme. Popped to perfection and sprinkled with the umami-rich taste of nutritional yeast, this popcorn offers a crunchy satisfaction that's not just delicious but also health-forward.

Servings: 4

Prepping Time: 5 minutes

Cook Time: 10 minutes

Difficulty: Easy

Ingredients:

- 1/2 cup popcorn kernels
- 1 tbsp coconut oil or olive oil
- 2 tbsp nutritional yeast

- ❖ 1/2 tsp salt (adjust to taste)

Step-by-Step Preparation:

- ✓ In a large pot, heat the oil over medium heat.
- ✓ Add a couple of popcorn kernels and cover.
- ✓ Once the kernels pop, add the rest of the popcorn kernels.
- ✓ Cover and shake the pot occasionally to ensure even popping and prevent burning.
- ✓ When the popping slows down, remove from heat.
- ✓ While warm, sprinkle with nutritional yeast and salt, tossing to coat evenly.
- ✓ Serve immediately.

Nutritional Facts: (Per serving)

- ❖ Calories: 90
- ❖ Cholesterol: 0mg
- ❖ Protein: 3g
- ❖ Carbohydrates: 15g
- ❖ Fiber: 3g
- ❖ Sugars: 0g
- ❖ Fat: 2.5g
- ❖ Sodium: 290mg

The "Light Popcorn with Nutritional Yeast" invites you to elevate your snacking experience, proving that light can be luscious. As you explore the culinary tapestry of may this snack serve as a delightful reminder of the beauty inherent in simplicity? With each crunchy bite infused with the savory goodness of nutritional yeast, you're treated to a dance of flavors that's as health-conscious as satisfying. So, gather your loved ones for movie night or indulge in a quiet moment of snacking bliss, knowing that you're treating yourself to the best of both worlds: taste and health.

Recipe 56: Chilled Melon Balls

Embrace the refreshing allure of "Chilled Melon Balls," a celebration of nature's simple yet vibrant bounty. While a departure from the beef stir fry narrative, this delightful dish harmoniously resonates with "Light and Luscious" theme. Extracted from succulent melons, these chilled orbs promise juicy sweetness and superb hydration, making them a sublime treat for warm days or when you crave something light and refreshing.

Servings: 4

Prepping Time: 15 minutes

Cook Time: 0 minutes

Difficulty: Easy

Ingredients:

- 1/2 cantaloupe melon
- 1/2 honeydew melon
- 1/2 watermelon
- Fresh mint leaves for garnish (optional)

- ❖ A sprinkle of sea salt (optional)

Step-by-Step Preparation:

- ✓ Using a melon baller, scoop out balls from each type of melon.
- ✓ Gently mix the melon balls in a large bowl.
- ✓ Refrigerate for at least 1 hour to chill.
- ✓ Before serving, sprinkle a pinch of sea salt on the melon balls for a contrasting flavor burst.
- ✓ Garnish with fresh mint leaves, if desired.
- ✓ Serve chilled in individual bowls.

Nutritional Facts: (Per serving)

- ❖ Calories: 60
- ❖ Cholesterol: 0mg
- ❖ Protein: 1g
- ❖ Carbohydrates: 15g
- ❖ Fiber: 1g
- ❖ Sugars: 13g
- ❖ Fat: 0.2g
- ❖ Sodium: 20mg (if added salt)

The "Chilled Melon Balls" transport you to a tranquil oasis where each bite offers a refreshing escape from the mundane. As you journey through let this dish epitomize the essence of light and lusciousness, showcasing how uncomplicated ingredients can bring sheer joy. Whether you're sunbathing by the pool, hosting a garden party, or simply seeking a refreshing snack, these melon orbs are bound to be the show's star. Dive into this symphony of natural sweetness, and let every bite remind you of the delightful pleasures of pure, unadulterated flavors. Cheers to nature's candy.

Recipe 57: Nutty Cocoa Energy Bites

Introducing the "Nutty Cocoa Energy Bites" – the perfect answer to sudden hunger pangs or when needing a quick energy boost. Departing from the beef stir fry trajectory, this delightful snack fits effortlessly into "Light and Luscious" theme. Crafted from wholesome ingredients like nuts and cocoa, these bites are decadently chocolate and power-packed, ensuring that energy and indulgence go hand in hand.

Servings: 10 bites

Prepping Time: 15 minutes

Cook Time: 0 minutes

Difficulty: Easy

Ingredients:

- 1 cup mixed nuts (almonds, walnuts, cashews)
- 2 tbsp cocoa powder
- 3 tbsp honey or maple syrup
- 1 tsp vanilla extract

- ❖ A pinch of salt
- ❖ Desiccated coconut for coating (optional)

Step-by-Step Preparation:

- ✓ In a food processor, blend the mixed nuts until finely ground.
- ✓ Add cocoa powder, honey or maple syrup, vanilla extract, and salt. Process until the mixture forms a sticky dough.
- ✓ Scoop out tablespoon-sized portions of the mixture and roll into balls.
- ✓ If desired, roll the balls in desiccated coconut for an added layer of flavor and texture.
- ✓ Place the bites on a tray and refrigerate for 1 hour to firm up.
- ✓ Store in an airtight container in the refrigerator.

Nutritional Facts: (Per serving)

- ❖ Calories: 100
- ❖ Cholesterol: 0mg
- ❖ Protein: 3g
- ❖ Carbohydrates: 8g
- ❖ Fiber: 2g
- ❖ Sugars: 5g
- ❖ Fat: 7g
- ❖ Sodium: 10mg

The "Nutty Cocoa Energy Bites" are a testament to the magic that unfolds when nutrition meets gourmet. As you explore the gastronomic wonders of let these little bites stand as an emblem of how easy and delightful health-conscious snacking can be. Every bite delivers a burst of energy, a splash of sweetness, and a comforting cocoa embrace, making it a snack you'd reach for repeatedly. Whether you're gearing up for a workout, battling mid-afternoon slumps, or seeking a post-dinner treat, these bites promise satisfaction without guilt. Celebrate the symphony of flavors and the power of natural ingredients with this delightful creation.

Recipe 58: Banana & Almond Smoothie

Moving away from the beef stir fry theme, this drink epitomizes "Light and Luscious" vision. With the natural sweetness of ripe bananas paired harmoniously with the nutty richness of almonds, this smoothie offers a refreshing yet filling experience, making it a perfect breakfast companion or an afternoon pick-me-up.

Servings: 2

Prepping Time: 5 minutes

Cook Time: 0 minutes

Difficulty: Easy

Ingredients:

- 2 ripe bananas
- 1/4 cup almond butter or almonds
- 2 cups almond milk (unsweetened)
- 1 tsp honey or maple syrup (optional)

- ❖ 1/2 tsp vanilla extract
- ❖ A sprinkle of ground cinnamon

Step-by-Step Preparation:

- ✓ In a blender, combine bananas, almond butter or almonds, almond milk, honey or maple syrup (if using), and vanilla extract.
- ✓ Blend until smooth and creamy.
- ✓ Taste and adjust sweetness or consistency, if necessary.
- ✓ Pour the smoothie into glasses, sprinkling the top with a dash of ground cinnamon.
- ✓ Serve immediately and enjoy.

Nutritional Facts: (Per serving)

- ❖ Calories: 250
- ❖ Cholesterol: 0mg
- ❖ Protein: 5g
- ❖ Carbohydrates: 35g
- ❖ Fiber: 5g
- ❖ Sugars: 18g
- ❖ Fat: 11g
- ❖ Sodium: 100mg

The "Banana & Almond Smoothie" invites you to bask in the sheer pleasure of flavors that nature generously offers. As you traverse the culinary delights of this smoothie stands as a beacon, illustrating that lightness and lusciousness can coexist in harmony. The amalgamation of banana's natural sweetness with almond's depth creates a drink that nurtures both the body and soul. Whether kick starting your morning or looking for a midday refreshment, let this smoothie remind you of the joys of simple, health-conscious indulgence. Here's to sipping on wellness.

Recipe 59: Rice Cakes with Avocado Spread

Elevate your snack game with the incredibly satisfying "Rice Cakes with Avocado Spread." Moving beyond the beef stir fry narrative, this delightful bite aligns perfectly with "Light and Luscious" theme. The crispiness of the rice cakes contrasts beautifully with the creamy richness of the avocado spread, resulting in a snack that's not just tantalizing to the taste buds but also wonderfully healthful.

Servings: 4

Prepping Time: 10 minutes

Cook Time: 0 minutes

Difficulty: Easy

Ingredients:

- 4 rice cakes
- 2 ripe avocados
- 1 tbsp lemon or lime juice
- Salt and pepper, to taste

- ❖ 1 tsp red chili flakes (optional)
- ❖ Fresh cilantro or parsley for garnish

Step-by-Step Preparation:

- ✓ Halve the avocados, remove the pit, and scoop the flesh into a bowl.
- ✓ Mash the avocado using a fork until relatively smooth.
- ✓ Add lemon or lime juice, salt, and pepper. Mix well.
- ✓ Spread a generous amount of the avocado mixture on each rice cake.
- ✓ Sprinkle with chili flakes if desired.
- ✓ Garnish with fresh cilantro or parsley.
- ✓ Serve immediately.

Nutritional Facts: (Per serving)

- ❖ Calories: 180
- ❖ Cholesterol: 0mg
- ❖ Protein: 3g
- ❖ Carbohydrates: 19g
- ❖ Fiber: 7g
- ❖ Sugars: 1g
- ❖ Fat: 11g
- ❖ Sodium: 15mg

Bask in the delightful interplay of textures and flavors with the "Rice Cakes with Avocado Spread," a snack that exemplifies the ethos of As you delve into the myriad of light and luscious offerings this chapter promises, let this recipe serve as a beacon of the beauty that lies in simplicity. Whether you need a quick breakfast, an afternoon pick-me-up, or an elegant appetizer for guests, these rice cakes stand ready to impress. Savor each crunchy, creamy bite, and revel in the knowledge that indulgence can be paired with wellness.

Recipe 60: Mixed Nuts with Dried Fruits

Venture into the wholesome world of "Mixed Nuts with Dried Fruits," a timeless snack that never ceases to satiate. Moving gracefully away from the beef stir fry theme, this handpicked mix aligns splendidly with "Light and Luscious" concept. With crunchy nuts meeting the chewy goodness of dried fruits, this blend satisfies cravings and offers a plethora of nutrients, making every handful a healthful indulgence.

Servings: 6

Prepping Time: 10 minutes

Cook Time: 0 minutes

Difficulty: Easy

Ingredients:

- 1 cup assorted nuts (almonds, walnuts, cashews, pecans)
- 1/2 cup dried fruits (raisins, apricots, cranberries, figs)
- A pinch of sea salt (optional)
- 1 tsp orange or lemon zest (optional)

Step-by-Step Preparation:

- ✓ In a large mixing bowl, combine the assorted nuts and dried fruits.
- ✓ If desired, sprinkle with sea salt and toss with the citrus zest for an added zing.
- ✓ Mix well, ensuring a good distribution of nuts and fruits.
- ✓ Store in an airtight container, and enjoy it as a delightful snack whenever hunger strikes.

Nutritional Facts: (Per serving)

- ❖ Calories: 190
- ❖ Cholesterol: 0mg
- ❖ Protein: 5g
- ❖ Carbohydrates: 18g
- ❖ Fiber: 3g
- ❖ Sugars: 10g
- ❖ Fat: 12g
- ❖ Sodium: 5mg (without added salt)

Embrace the simplistic elegance of the "Mixed Nuts with Dried Fruits," a snack that embodies the heart of as you uncover the treasures within this chapter, this mix showcases the beauty of nature's offerings in their purest form. Every bite delivers a symphony of textures and flavors, reminding us of the joys of mindful munching. This blend celebrates the harmony of nutrition and taste, perfect for on-the-go, midday breaks, or even as a topping for breakfast bowls. Dive deep into the joys of simple yet profound pleasures, and remember that the best indulgences often come in the most natural forms. Cheers to wholesome snacking.

Chapter 07: Soul-Warming Soups with a Healthy Twist

Recipe 61: Hearty Lentil & Vegetable Soup

Dive into the aromatic depths of "Hearty Lentil & Vegetable Soup," a perfect bowl of comfort for those cooler days or when your soul craves a touch of warmth. Distancing from the beef stir fry theme; this soup harmoniously captures narrative of "Soul-Warming Soups with a Healthy Twist." With nutrient-dense lentils paired seamlessly with a medley of vibrant vegetables, this soup offers both satiety and a bouquet of flavors in every spoonful.

Servings: 6

Prepping Time: 15 minutes

Cook Time: 40 minutes

Difficulty: Moderate

Ingredients:

- 1 cup green or brown lentils, rinsed
- 1 onion, diced

- ❖ 2 carrots, sliced
- ❖ 2 celery stalks, chopped
- ❖ 3 garlic cloves, minced
- ❖ 6 cups vegetable broth
- ❖ 1 can (14 oz) diced tomatoes
- ❖ 2 bay leaves
- ❖ 1 tsp dried thyme
- ❖ Salt and pepper to taste
- ❖ 2 tbsp olive oil
- ❖ Fresh parsley for garnish

Step-by-Step Preparation:

- ✓ In a large pot, heat olive oil over medium heat. Add onions, carrots, and celery, sautéing until softened.
- ✓ Add the minced garlic and sauté for another 2 minutes until fragrant.
- ✓ Pour in the vegetable broth, lentils, diced tomatoes, bay leaves, and thyme.
- ✓ Bring to a boil, then reduce heat, cover, and simmer for 30 minutes or until lentils are tender.
- ✓ Season with salt and pepper according to preference.
- ✓ Once cooked, remove bay leaves.
- ✓ Ladle into bowls and garnish with fresh parsley.

Nutritional Facts: (Per serving)

- ❖ Calories: 210
- ❖ Protein: 11g
- ❖ Carbohydrates: 32g
- ❖ Fiber: 13g
- ❖ Sugars: 6g
- ❖ Fat: 4g
- ❖ Sodium: 460mg

The "Hearty Lentil & Vegetable Soup" invites you to experience the joys of soulful dining, where every bite nurtures both the body and spirit. As you immerse yourself in the offerings of Chapter 07, this soup stands as a testament to the profound beauty that arises when health meets comfort.

Recipe 62: Tomato Basil Bliss Soup

Embrace the timeless allure of the "Tomato Basil Bliss Soup," a heartwarming concoction that speaks to the soul. Venturing beyond the beef stir fry narrative, this culinary delight is a prime representation of Chapter 07's "Soul-Warming Soups with a Healthy Twist." The rich, tangy notes of tomatoes, complemented by the aromatic essence of basil, create a soup that is both nostalgic and refreshing, resonating with memories of comforting home-cooked meals.

Servings: 4

Prepping Time: 10 minutes

Cook Time: 30 minutes

Difficulty: Easy

Ingredients:

- 6 ripe tomatoes, diced
- 1 onion, finely chopped

- ❖ 3 cloves garlic, minced
- ❖ 2 cups vegetable broth
- ❖ 1/4 cup fresh basil, finely chopped
- ❖ 2 tbsp olive oil
- ❖ 1/2 cup cream or coconut milk (for a vegan twist)
- ❖ Salt and pepper to taste
- ❖ Grated Parmesan or vegan cheese for garnish (optional)

Step-by-Step Preparation:

- ✓ In a pot, heat olive oil and sauté onions until translucent.
- ✓ Introduce garlic and continue sautéing until aromatic.
- ✓ Add tomatoes and cook until they become soft and pulpy.
- ✓ Incorporate the vegetable broth and allow the mixture to come to a simmer.
- ✓ Stir in the fresh basil, salt, and pepper. Continue to simmer for about 20 minutes.
- ✓ Puree the mixture using a blender or immersion blender to achieve a smooth consistency.
- ✓ Return the soup to the pot and stir in cream or coconut milk, warming gently.
- ✓ Serve garnished with grated Parmesan or vegan cheese, if desired.

Nutritional Facts: (Per serving)

- ❖ Calories: 180
- ❖ Cholesterol: 25mg (using cream)
- ❖ Protein: 4g
- ❖ Carbohydrates: 16g
- ❖ Fiber: 3g
- ❖ Sugars: 9g
- ❖ Fat: 11g (varies with choice of cream or milk)
- ❖ Sodium: 390mg

The "Tomato Basil Bliss Soup" encapsulates the essence of warmth, comfort, and culinary tradition. As you delve deeper into Chapter 07, may this dish be a gentle reminder of the transformative power of simple ingredients combined with love and passion. Whether you're looking for a cozy meal on a rainy evening or a nourishing dish to share with loved ones, this soup is a beacon of homely comfort.

Recipe 63: Creamy Butternut Squash & Carrot Soup

As the seasons shift and the temperature drops, nothing provides comfort like a bowl of warm soup. The Creamy Butternut Squash & Carrot Soup offers a velvety texture and vibrant flavors. Combining the natural sweetness of butternut squash and carrot with the richness of cream, this soup promises to warm your soul from the inside out.

Servings: 4

Prepping Time: 15 minutes

Cook Time: 30 minutes

Difficulty: Easy

Ingredients:

- 1 medium butternut squash, peeled and cubed
- 3 large carrots, peeled and chopped
- 1 onion, finely chopped
- 2 cloves of garlic, minced
- 4 cups vegetable broth

- ❖ 1 cup heavy cream
- ❖ 1 teaspoon salt
- ❖ 1/2 teaspoon black pepper
- ❖ 1/2 teaspoon nutmeg
- ❖ 2 tablespoons olive oil
- ❖ Fresh parsley for garnish

Step-by-Step Preparation:

- ✓ In a large pot, heat olive oil over medium heat. Add onions and garlic, and sauté until translucent.
- ✓ Add the butternut squash, carrots, salt, pepper, and nutmeg to the pot. Stir well.
- ✓ Pour in the vegetable broth, ensuring the vegetables are submerged. Bring to a boil.
- ✓ Reduce the heat, cover, and simmer for 20-25 minutes or until the vegetables are tender.
- ✓ Using a blender or immersion blender, puree the mixture until smooth.
- ✓ Return the soup to the pot and stir in the heavy cream. Heat gently until warmed through.
- ✓ Taste and adjust seasoning if necessary.
- ✓ Serve hot, garnished with fresh parsley.

Nutritional Facts (Per serving):

- ❖ Calories: 280 kcal
- ❖ Protein: 4g
- ❖ Carbs: 30g
- ❖ Dietary Fiber: 6g
- ❖ Sugars: 8g
- ❖ Fat: 18g
- ❖ Saturated Fat: 9g
- ❖ Sodium: 890mg

While a beef stir fry might be the star of many dinner tables, this Creamy Butternut Squash and Carrot Soup proves that the side dishes or starters can sometimes outshine the mains. Infused with hearty flavors and brimming with nutritional benefits, this soup isn't just about warmth and comfort; it's a testament to how simple ingredients, combined thoughtfully, can create a gastronomic masterpiece.

Recipe 64: Clear Broth with Greens & Tofu

In the realm of soul-warming soups, diversity is the key. While beef stir-fry may capture the limelight in the Clear Broth with Greens & Tofu stands as its humble yet profound counterpart. Light, revitalizing, and brimming with fresh greens' verdant goodness, this soup melds with silken tofu chunks to offer a serene culinary experience. This Asian-inspired delicacy, set against the backdrop of our chapter on hearty, comforting dishes, introduces a touch of gentle elegance, reaffirming that warmth can be bold and delicate.

Servings: 4

Prepping Time: 10 minutes

Cook Time: 20 minutes

Difficulty: Easy

Ingredients:

- 4 cups clear vegetable broth
- 2 cups assorted greens (like baby spinach, kale, choy sum)
- 1 block of firm tofu, cubed

- ❖ 2 cloves garlic, minced
- ❖ 1 tablespoon light soy sauce
- ❖ 1 teaspoon sesame oil
- ❖ Dash of white pepper
- ❖ Fresh coriander for garnish

Step-by-Step Preparation:

- ✓ Warm the sesame oil in a pot over medium heat. Sauté the garlic till fragrant.
- ✓ Pour in the clear vegetable broth and bring to a gentle simmer.
- ✓ Add the light soy sauce and a dash of white pepper.
- ✓ Gently place the tofu cubes into the broth, letting them simmer for about 8 minutes.
- ✓ Introduce the assorted greens and let them wilt for approximately 2-3 minutes.
- ✓ Once cooked, turn off the heat and serve the broth in individual bowls.
- ✓ Garnish with fresh coriander before serving.

Nutritional Facts (Per serving):

- ❖ Calories: 100 kcal
- ❖ Protein: 9g
- ❖ Carbs: 4g
- ❖ Dietary Fiber: 1g
- ❖ Sugars: 1g
- ❖ Fat: 5g
- ❖ Saturated Fat: 0.5g
- ❖ Sodium: 650mg

Against the rich tapestry of flavors showcased in the Clear Broth with Greens & Tofu emerges as a testimony to the grace of simplicity. It's clear, shimmering broth serves as a canvas to the dance of tender greens and creamy tofu, delivering nourishment and a refreshing palate cleanse. This recipe isn't just about providing warmth; it celebrates the beauty of minimalism, the understated elegance of pure ingredients, and the harmony they bring when combined. As you savor each spoonful, let it remind you of the infinite ways food warms our hearts and souls. Here's to finding comfort in every culinary corner.

Recipe 65: Spinach & White Bean Soup

In the vibrant array of comforting soups in our Spinach and White Bean Soup emerges as a green gem. This soup combines the earthy notes of spinach with the hearty texture of white beans, resulting in a pot of nourishment that's both soul-warming and rejuvenating. This humble concoction stands tall amidst an array of beef stir-fry dishes, showcasing how plant-based ingredients can pack a punch in comfort foods.

Servings: 4

Prepping Time: 10 minutes

Cook Time: 25 minutes

Difficulty: Easy

Ingredients:

- 4 cups vegetable broth
- 2 cups fresh spinach, chopped
- 1 can (15 oz) white beans, drained and rinsed
- 1 medium onion, diced
- 3 cloves garlic, minced

- 1 teaspoon olive oil
- 1/2 teaspoon dried thyme
- Salt and pepper to taste
- Grated Parmesan for garnish (optional)

Step-by-Step Preparation:

- In a soup pot, heat the olive oil over medium flame. Sauté onions and garlic until translucent.
- Add the white beans to the pot, stirring to combine.
- Pour in the vegetable broth and bring the mixture to a boil.
- Add dried thyme, salt, and pepper, and let the soup simmer for 15 minutes.
- Incorporate the chopped spinach and continue to simmer until the spinach is wilted and tender, about 5 minutes.
- Taste and adjust seasoning if necessary.
- Serve hot, garnishing with a sprinkle of grated Parmesan if desired.

Nutritional Facts (Per serving):

- Calories: 210 kcal
- Protein: 12g
- Carbs: 37g
- Dietary Fiber: 9g
- Sugars: 3g
- Fat: 2g
- Saturated Fat: 0.5g
- Sodium: 680mg

Amid the hearty and robust flavors of the Spinach & White Bean Soup introduces a breath of fresh air. Its delicate balance between the soft beans and vibrant spinach offers a culinary experience that's both soothing and refreshing. As you dive into this bowl of wholesome goodness, let it serve as a testament to the versatility of soups, proving that comfort can come in lighter, greener packages. With each spoonful, discover a world where taste, health, and warmth coalesce seamlessly. Enjoy the symphony of flavors and let this soup, though gentle, leave an indelible mark on your culinary journey.

Recipe 66: Chilled Cucumber & Dill Soup

In the vibrant array of comforting soups in our Spinach and White Bean Soup emerges as a green gem. This soup combines the earthy notes of spinach with the hearty texture of white beans, resulting in a pot of nourishment that's both soul-warming and rejuvenating. This humble concoction stands tall amidst an array of beef stir-fry dishes, showcasing how plant-based ingredients can pack a punch in comfort foods.

Servings: 4

Prepping Time: 10 minutes

Cook Time: 25 minutes

Difficulty: Easy

Ingredients:

- 4 cups vegetable broth
- 2 cups fresh spinach, chopped
- 1 can (15 oz) white beans, drained and rinsed
- 1 medium onion, diced

- ❖ 3 cloves garlic, minced
- ❖ 1 teaspoon olive oil
- ❖ 1/2 teaspoon dried thyme
- ❖ Salt and pepper to taste
- ❖ Grated Parmesan for garnish (optional)

Step-by-Step Preparation:

- ✓ In a soup pot, heat the olive oil over medium flame. Sauté onions and garlic until translucent.
- ✓ Add the white beans to the pot, stirring to combine.
- ✓ Pour in the vegetable broth and bring the mixture to a boil.
- ✓ Add dried thyme, salt, and pepper, and let the soup simmer for 15 minutes.
- ✓ Incorporate the chopped spinach and continue to simmer until the spinach is wilted and tender, about 5 minutes.
- ✓ Taste and adjust seasoning if necessary.
- ✓ Serve hot, garnishing with a sprinkle of grated Parmesan if desired.

Nutritional Facts (Per serving):

- ❖ Calories: 210 kcal
- ❖ Protein: 12g
- ❖ Carbs: 37g
- ❖ Dietary Fiber: 9g
- ❖ Sugars: 3g
- ❖ Fat: 2g
- ❖ Saturated Fat: 0.5g
- ❖ Sodium: 680mg

Amid the hearty and robust flavors of the Spinach & White Bean Soup introduces a breath of fresh air. Its delicate balance between the soft beans and vibrant spinach offers a culinary experience that's both soothing and refreshing. As you dive into this bowl of wholesome goodness, let it serve as a testament to the versatility of soups, proving that comfort can come in lighter, greener packages. With each spoonful, discover a world where taste, health, and warmth coalesce seamlessly. Enjoy the symphony of flavors and let this soup, though gentle, leave an indelible mark on your culinary journey.

Recipe 67: Spicy Pumpkin & Ginger Soup

Nestled amidst the rich flavors of beef stir-fry in is the Spicy Pumpkin & Ginger Soup, a blend that promises fiery warmth with each spoonful. This soup marries the creamy texture of pumpkin with the zesty kick of ginger, creating a harmonious fusion that's both comforting and refreshing. While our chapter brims with hearty dishes, this soup adds a touch of spirited zest, illuminating the versatility of comfort foods.

Servings: 4

Prepping Time: 15 minutes

Cook Time: 30 minutes

Difficulty: Moderate

Ingredients:

- 4 cups pumpkin puree
- 1 onion, finely chopped
- 2 cloves garlic, minced
- 2-inch piece of fresh ginger, grated

- ❖ 4 cups vegetable broth
- ❖ 1 can (13.5 oz) coconut milk
- ❖ 1 teaspoon ground cayenne pepper
- ❖ Salt and pepper to taste
- ❖ Olive oil for sautéing
- ❖ Fresh coriander for garnish

Step-by-Step Preparation:

- ✓ In a large pot, heat olive oil over medium flame. Add onions and garlic, sautéing until translucent.
- ✓ Introduce the grated ginger and sauté for another minute until aromatic.
- ✓ Pour in the vegetable broth, followed by the pumpkin puree, stirring well.
- ✓ Bring the mixture to a boil, and then lower the heat, allowing it to simmer for 20 minutes.
- ✓ Stir in the coconut milk, cayenne pepper, salt, and pepper, simmering for 10 minutes.
- ✓ Using an immersion blender, blend the soup until smooth (optional).
- ✓ Serve hot, garnished with fresh coriander.

Nutritional Facts (Per serving):

- ❖ Calories: 250 kcal
- ❖ Protein: 5g
- ❖ Carbs: 30g
- ❖ Dietary Fiber: 6g
- ❖ Sugars: 8g
- ❖ Fat: 15g
- ❖ Saturated Fat: 12g
- ❖ Sodium: 890mg

The Spicy Pumpkin & Ginger Soup offers a compelling escape in a teeming with robust flavors. Each sip is a dance of contrasts - the smoothness of pumpkin playing off against the sharpness of ginger. This soup doesn't just warm the body but also invigorates the senses. Its vibrant character is a reminder that even in the realm of comfort, there's room for excitement and dynamism. As you indulge in its spicy embrace, let it rekindle the joy of discovering unexpected culinary delights.

Recipe 68: Red Beet Borscht

Amidst the tantalizing beef stir-fry dishes of the Red Beet Borscht emerges like a ruby, exuding old-world charm. This traditional Eastern European soup is a symphony of earthy beetroot flavors, heightened with aromatic spices and herbs. In our Soul-Warming Soups with a Healthy Twist collection, this borscht stands as a testament to the timeless allure of classic recipes that have warmed countless hearts over generations.

Servings: 4

Prepping Time: 20 minutes

Cook Time: 40 minutes

Difficulty: Moderate

Ingredients:

- 3 medium-sized beets, peeled and grated
- 1 onion, finely chopped
- 2 cloves garlic, minced
- 4 cups beef or vegetable broth

- ❖ 2 medium-sized potatoes, diced
- ❖ 1 carrot, grated
- ❖ 2 tablespoons tomato paste
- ❖ 1 tablespoon vinegar
- ❖ 1 teaspoon sugar
- ❖ Salt and pepper to taste
- ❖ Sour cream and dill for garnish

Step-by-Step Preparation:

- ✓ In a large pot, sauté onions and garlic until translucent.
- ✓ Add the grated beets, carrot, and tomato paste, stirring well.
- ✓ Pour in the broth and bring the mixture to a boil.
- ✓ Add the diced potatoes, reducing the heat to let the soup simmer.
- ✓ After 20 minutes, stir in the vinegar, sugar, salt, and pepper.
- ✓ Let the soup simmer for 15-20 minutes or until all vegetables are tender.
- ✓ Adjust the seasoning as required.
- ✓ Serve hot, topped with a dollop of sour cream and a sprinkle of fresh dill.

Nutritional Facts (Per serving):

- ❖ Calories: 180 kcal
- ❖ Protein: 5g
- ❖ Carbs: 38g
- ❖ Dietary Fiber: 6g
- ❖ Sugars: 10g
- ❖ Fat: 1g
- ❖ Saturated Fat: 0.2g
- ❖ Sodium: 830mg

In the warmth of the Red Beet Borscht isn't merely another soup; it's a journey through history, carrying with it tales of grandmothers' kitchens and festive family gatherings. Its deep, crimson hue and rich flavor profile serve as a poignant reminder of the power of traditional recipes to transcend time. As you savor its earthy depths, let it transport you to a cozy cottage, with the snow gently falling outside and the room aglow with shared memories and laughter.

Recipe 69: Heartwarming Mushroom & Barley Soup

Dominated by the sumptuous allure of beef stir-fry dishes, is enriched further by our Heartwarming Mushroom and Barley Soup. This soup is an ode to the comforting and earthy symphony of mushrooms, harmonized with the chewy texture of barley grains. It's a bowl that exudes rustic charm and promises warmth that seems to seep into your soul, providing solace on chilly days.

Servings: 4

Prepping Time: 15 minutes

Cook Time: 50 minutes

Difficulty: Moderate

Ingredients:

- 1 cup pearl barley
- 3 cups mixed mushrooms, sliced (like cremini, shiitake, portobello)
- 1 onion, diced

- 2 cloves garlic, minced
- 5 cups vegetable or chicken broth
- 2 tablespoons olive oil
- 1 teaspoon dried thyme
- Salt and pepper to taste
- Fresh parsley for garnish

Step-by-Step Preparation:

- In a large pot, heat the olive oil over medium flame. Sauté onions and garlic until translucent.
- Add the sliced mushrooms, cooking until they release their juices and turn golden.
- Stir in the pearl barley, ensuring it's well-coated with the mushroom mixture.
- Pour in the broth and bring the concoction to a boil.
- Add thyme, salt, and pepper. Reduce heat, letting the soup simmer for 40-45 minutes or until barley is tender.
- Adjust seasonings if needed.
- Serve piping hot, garnished with freshly chopped parsley.

Nutritional Facts (Per serving):

- Calories: 220 kcal
- Protein: 8g
- Carbs: 45g
- Dietary Fiber: 10g
- Sugars: 4g
- Fat: 4g
- Saturated Fat: 0.5g
- Sodium: 760mg

The Heartwarming Mushroom & Barley Soup is a heartfelt embrace in a bowl. Amidst the vibrant tapestry of this soup is a testament to the straightforward, timeless appeal of earthy ingredients melded with care. Its depth of flavors is reminiscent of old-world kitchens, where every dish was a story and every flavor a cherished memory. As you immerse yourself in its rich broth and savor the dance of mushrooms and barley on your palate, let it transport you to a place of warmth, nostalgia, and pure culinary joy.

Recipe 70: Refreshing Gazpacho

While showcases the rich flavors of beef stir-fry, it also pays homage to the varied tapestry of soups that comfort in different ways. The Refreshing Gazpacho is an arresting interlude, a chilled Spanish classic that proves warmth can be felt even in the most incredible dishes. Bursting with fresh vegetables and a splash of tang, this vibrant soup invites you to experience comfort in a refreshingly cold embrace.

Servings: 4

Prepping Time: 20 minutes

Cook Time: No cook time. Chill for 3 hours

Difficulty: Easy

Ingredients:

- 6 ripe tomatoes, diced
- 1 cucumber, peeled and diced
- 1 bell pepper, diced
- 1 small red onion, diced

- ❖ 2 cloves garlic, minced
- ❖ 3 cups tomato juice
- ❖ 2 tablespoons red wine vinegar
- ❖ 2 tablespoons olive oil
- ❖ Salt and pepper to taste
- ❖ Fresh basil for garnish

Step-by-Step Preparation:

- ✓ Combine tomatoes, cucumber, bell pepper, red onion, and garlic in a blender. Blend until slightly chunky or to desired consistency.
- ✓ Transfer the blended mixture to a large bowl.
- ✓ Add the tomato juice, red wine vinegar, olive oil, salt, and pepper. Mix well.
- ✓ Cover the bowl and refrigerate for at least 3 hours, allowing flavors to meld together.
- ✓ Serve chilled, garnished with fresh basil leaves.

Nutritional Facts (Per serving):

- ❖ Calories: 130 kcal
- ❖ Protein: 3g
- ❖ Carbs: 23g
- ❖ Dietary Fiber: 4g
- ❖ Sugars: 13g
- ❖ Fat: 5g
- ❖ Saturated Fat: 0.7g
- ❖ Sodium: 480mg

Amid the robust and hearty flavors of the Refreshing Gazpacho emerges as a delightful paradox. With its riot of colors and flavors, this chilled soup speaks to the soul in gentle whispers, offering a unique kind of refreshing and cooling comfort. Each spoonful is a dance of garden-fresh ingredients, beckoning you to savor simplicity in its most exquisite form. As you dive into this culinary masterpiece, let it be a testament to how comfort can be perceived and savored. Here's celebrating the magic of dishes that, though cold in temperature, warm the heart in the most unexpected ways.

Chapter 08: Appetizers to Begin with a Beat

Recipe 71: Cherry Tomato & Basil Skewers

Among these starters, the Cherry Tomato & Basil Skewers stand out for their vibrant appearance and their burst of freshness with each bite. These skewers, juxtaposed amidst beef stir-fry delights, exemplify that appetizers needn't be elaborate to be memorable; sometimes, when paired thoughtfully, the simplest ingredients can create the most harmonious preludes.

Servings: 4

Prepping Time: 10 minutes

Cook Time: No cook time

Difficulty: Easy

Ingredients:

- ❖ 16 cherry tomatoes

- ❖ 16 fresh basil leaves
- ❖ 1 cup fresh mozzarella balls
- ❖ 2 tablespoons olive oil
- ❖ 1 tablespoon balsamic reduction
- ❖ Salt and pepper to taste
- ❖ Wooden skewers

Step-by-Step Preparation:

- ✓ Start by assembling your skewers: thread a cherry tomato, followed by a basil leaf, and then a mozzarella ball. Repeat this sequence until the skewer is filled.
- ✓ Prepare all skewers similarly.
- ✓ Arrange the skewers on a serving platter.
- ✓ Drizzle olive oil and balsamic reduction over the skewers.
- ✓ Season with salt and pepper.
- ✓ Serve immediately, ensuring each skewer has a tomato, basil, and mozzarella mix.

Nutritional Facts (Per serving):

- ❖ Calories: 150 kcal
- ❖ Protein: 7g
- ❖ Carbs: 3g
- ❖ Dietary Fiber: 1g
- ❖ Sugars: 2g
- ❖ Fat: 12g
- ❖ Saturated Fat: 4g
- ❖ Sodium: 150mg

Amid the culinary crescendos of the Cherry Tomato & Basil Skewers strike a chord of simplicity, elegance, and flavor. These skewers, juxtaposing juicy tomatoes, fragrant basil, and creamy mozzarella, become a sensory delight, reminding us that the best appetizers often whet the appetite without overwhelming the senses. As you indulge in these bite-sized wonders, let them be a testament to the magic of straightforward ingredients harmoniously intertwined.

Recipe 72: Zucchini Rolls with Hummus & Peppers

The stage with appetizers that resonate with culinary rhythm the Zucchini Rolls with Hummus and peppers stand out as a musical prelude. This dish, layered with textures and flavors, harmonizes the delicate taste of zucchini with the rich depth of hummus and the zesty kick of peppers. While nestled among beef stir-fry creations, these rolls champion the notion that sometimes, the most captivating beginnings are wrapped in elegance and simplicity.

Servings: 4

Prepping Time: 20 minutes

Cook Time: 5 minutes

Difficulty: Moderate

Ingredients:

- ❖ 2 large zucchinis, thinly sliced lengthwise
- ❖ 1 cup hummus

- ❖ 1/2 cup roasted red peppers, thinly sliced
- ❖ 2 tablespoons olive oil
- ❖ Salt and pepper to taste
- ❖ Fresh parsley for garnish

Step-by-Step Preparation:

- ✓ Heat a grill pan or skillet over medium heat and brush with olive oil.
- ✓ Grill the zucchini slices for about 2 minutes on each side until tender but not overly soft.
- ✓ Lay each grilled zucchini slice flat and spread a thin layer of hummus over it.
- ✓ Place a few slices of roasted red pepper at one end of the zucchini.
- ✓ Gently roll the zucchini, enclosing the hummus and peppers.
- ✓ Secure with a toothpick if necessary.
- ✓ Arrange on a platter, season with salt and pepper, and garnish with fresh parsley.

Nutritional Facts (Per serving):

- ❖ Calories: 140 kcal
- ❖ Protein: 4g
- ❖ Carbs: 10g
- ❖ Dietary Fiber: 3g
- ❖ Sugars: 2g
- ❖ Fat: 10g
- ❖ Saturated Fat: 1.5g
- ❖ Sodium: 180mg

In the dynamic ensemble of the Zucchini Rolls with Hummus and peppers play a gentle yet unforgettable tune? With their delicate wraps and flavorful fillings, these rolls remind us that appetizers can be refined and satiating. The dance of creamy hummus with charred zucchini and vibrant peppers creates an appetizer that's as visually appealing as it is delicious. Let these rolls set the tone as you embark on this culinary journey, promising an experience filled with flavor nuances and delightful surprises. After all, every memorable feast begins with a promise of what's to come, and these rolls deliver that promise with every bite.

Recipe 73: Mini Spinach & Feta Tarts

While pulses with the robust rhythm of beef stir-fry masterpieces, it also gracefully opens the floor to diverse culinary beats. Among them, the Mini Spinach & Feta Tarts make a graceful entrance. These bite-sized delights, encapsulating the rich blend of creamy feta and verdant spinach, offer a symphony of flavors and textures. Set against a backdrop of hearty appetizers, these tarts shine, echoing the sentiment that true gastronomic wonders often come in the most petite packages.

Servings: 12 mini tarts

Prepping Time: 20 minutes

Cook Time: 25 minutes

Difficulty: Moderate

Ingredients:

- 1 pre-rolled puff pastry sheet
- 1 cup fresh spinach, chopped
- 1/2 cup feta cheese, crumbled
- 1 small onion, finely chopped
- 2 cloves garlic, minced

- ❖ 1 egg, beaten
- ❖ 1 tablespoon olive oil
- ❖ Salt and pepper to taste
- ❖ Fresh dill for garnish

Step-by-Step Preparation:

- ✓ Preheat the oven to 375°F (190°C) and lightly grease a mini muffin tin.
- ✓ In a skillet, heat olive oil over medium heat. Sauté onions and garlic until translucent.
- ✓ Add the chopped spinach, cooking until wilted.
- ✓ Remove from heat and let it cool. Once cooled, mix in the crumbled feta cheese.
- ✓ Season with salt and pepper.
- ✓ Roll out the puff pastry and cut into small circles, fitting them into the muffin tin to form mini tart shells.
- ✓ Fill each shell with the spinach and feta mixture.
- ✓ Brush the edges of the pastry with the beaten egg.
- ✓ Bake for 20-25 minutes or until golden brown.
- ✓ Garnish with fresh dill before serving.

Nutritional Facts (Per serving):

- ❖ Calories: 110 kcal
- ❖ Protein: 3g
- ❖ Carbs: 8g
- ❖ Dietary Fiber: 1g
- ❖ Sugars: 1g
- ❖ Fat: 7g
- ❖ Saturated Fat: 2.5g
- ❖ Sodium: 160mg

Amid the resonant beats of the Mini Spinach & Feta Tarts stand as a harmonious interlude blending tradition with contemporary flair. Their delicate, flaky crust cradling a heart of sumptuous filling is reminiscent of age-old flavors, reimagined for the modern palate. As you bite, let these tarts transport you to Mediterranean coasts, where every dish tells a tale. Here's to the beauty of small packages, delivering big on flavor and memory, ensuring that the start of any culinary experience is as memorable as its grand finale.

Recipe 74: Guacamole & Salsa Dip Duo

In the dynamic playlist of the Guacamole & Salsa Dip Duo makes its mark as a vibrant duet. Set against beef stir-fry compositions, this dip duo serenades the palate with a spicy, tangy, and creamy melody. Capturing the essence of fresh ingredients and the spirited heart of Latin culinary traditions, these dips provide a refreshing counterpoint, ensuring that the appetizer stage is set with vivacity and zest.

Servings: 6

Prepping Time: 20 minutes

Cook Time: No cook time

Difficulty: Easy

Ingredients:

- 3 ripe avocados, pitted and mashed
- 2 tomatoes, finely chopped
- 1 red onion, finely chopped
- 2 jalapeños, seeded and minced
- 2 cloves garlic, minced
- Juice of 2 limes
- 1/2 cup fresh cilantro, chopped

- ❖ Salt and pepper to taste

Step-by-Step Preparation:

- ✓ Combine mashed avocados, half of the chopped tomatoes, half of the red onion, one minced jalapeño, one minced garlic clove, and juice of one lime. Mix well to form the Guacamole.
- ✓ Season with salt and pepper; they are adjusting to taste. Garnish with some chopped cilantro.
- ✓ In another bowl, mix the remaining tomatoes, red onion, jalapeño, garlic, and juice of the other lime to create the salsa.
- ✓ Stir in half of the chopped cilantro and season with salt and pepper.
- ✓ Serve the Guacamole and salsa with your choice of tortilla chips.

Nutritional Facts (Per serving):

- ❖ Calories: 150 kcal
- ❖ Protein: 3g
- ❖ Carbs: 10g
- ❖ Dietary Fiber: 7g
- ❖ Sugars: 2g
- ❖ Fat: 12g
- ❖ Saturated Fat: 2g
- ❖ Sodium: 10mg

Amidst the culinary beats of the Guacamole and salsa Dip Duo emerge as a jubilant celebration of fresh flavors. Their harmonious blend of textures and tastes offers a lively prelude, inviting guests to dive into the culinary treasures that wait. As each dip graces your palate, be it the creamy allure of the Guacamole or the fiery zest of the salsa, it transports you to sun-kissed terrains where food is both an art and a heartwarming ritual. Here's to appetizers that not only tantalize the taste buds but also weave stories of traditions, landscapes, and shared joys. Dive in, and let this duo set the tone for an unforgettable gastronomic journey.

Recipe 75: Light Mozzarella & Olive Tapenade

In culinary orchestra, where beef stir-fry plays the lead, the Light Mozzarella & Olive Tapenade emerges as a delightful overture. This dish seamlessly marries the creamy subtlety of mozzarella with the salty depth of olives, creating an understated and impactful appetizer. As we journey through appetizers designed to set the rhythm, this tapenade offers a nuanced note, promising a menu replete with intensity and elegance.

Servings: 6

Prepping Time: 15 minutes

Cook Time: No cook time

Difficulty: Easy

Ingredients:

- 1 cup black and green olives, pitted and chopped
- 1/2 cup fresh mozzarella balls
- 2 cloves garlic, minced
- 2 tablespoons capers, drained
- 3 tablespoons olive oil

- ❖ Zest of 1 lemon
- ❖ Fresh parsley, finely chopped
- ❖ Salt and pepper to taste
- ❖ Crusty bread or crackers for serving

Step-by-Step Preparation:

- ✓ Combine olives, garlic, capers, olive oil, and lemon zest in a food processor. Pulse until a coarse paste forms.
- ✓ Season the tapenade with salt and pepper, adjusting to your preference.
- ✓ Transfer the tapenade to a serving dish.
- ✓ Intersperse the tapenade with fresh mozzarella balls.
- ✓ Garnish with finely chopped parsley.
- ✓ Serve with slices of crusty bread or your favorite crackers.

Nutritional Facts (Per serving):

- ❖ Calories: 140 kcal
- ❖ Protein: 4g
- ❖ Carbs: 3g
- ❖ Dietary Fiber: 1g
- ❖ Sugars: 1g
- ❖ Fat: 12g
- ❖ Saturated Fat: 3g
- ❖ Sodium: 400mg

The Light Mozzarella & Olive Tapenade is a culinary sonnet in its delicate interplay of flavors and textures sings of Mediterranean shores and sunlit picnics. Every bite is a delightful contrast — the olives' saltiness meeting the mozzarella's gentle creaminess. This appetizer reminds us that the most profound flavors are sometimes born from simplicity and thoughtful pairing. As you savor its rich yet light essence, let it set the tempo for the gastronomic symphony that waits. Here's to beginnings that, though subtle, echo long after the last note, promising a meal that dances gracefully between tradition and innovation.

Recipe 76: Stuffed Grape Leaves with Rice & Herbs

Within the resonant pages of where beef stir-fry sets a vigorous pace, the Stuffed Grape Leaves with Rice & Herbs bring a rhythmic and traditional counterpoint. These delicate parcels, a Mediterranean and Middle Eastern cuisine staple, encapsulate a medley of fragrant rice and herbs within the tender embrace of grape leaves. As appetizers that simultaneously captivate and soothe, they offer a harmonious prelude to the culinary concert ahead.

Servings: 6

Prepping Time: 30 minutes

Cook Time: 40 minutes

Difficulty: Intermediate

Ingredients:

- ❖ 30 grape leaves, jarred or fresh
- ❖ 1 cup short-grain rice, uncooked
- ❖ 1/4 cup fresh parsley, finely chopped
- ❖ 2 tablespoons fresh mint, finely chopped

- ❖ 1 small onion, finely diced
- ❖ 3 tablespoons olive oil
- ❖ Juice of 1 lemon
- ❖ Salt and pepper to taste
- ❖ 2 cups vegetable broth

Step-by-Step Preparation:

- ✓ Rinse grape leaves thoroughly and pat dry.
- ✓ Mix rice, parsley, mint, onion, lemon juice, salt, pepper, and half the olive oil in a mixing bowl.
- ✓ Place a grape leaf on a flat surface, shiny side down. Place a small spoonful of the rice mixture in the center.
- ✓ Fold the sides of the grape leaf inwards, then roll tightly to form a small cylindrical parcel.
- ✓ Repeat with all grape leaves and filling.
- ✓ Arrange the stuffed leaves closely together in a deep pan, seam side down.
- ✓ Pour vegetable broth and the remaining olive oil over the grape leaves.
- ✓ Bring to a simmer and cook, covered, for 40 minutes or until rice is tender.
- ✓ Allow to cool slightly before serving.

Nutritional Facts (Per serving):

- ❖ Calories: 190 kcal
- ❖ Protein: 3g
- ❖ Carbs: 35g
- ❖ Dietary Fiber: 2g
- ❖ Sugars: 1g
- ❖ Fat: 5g
- ❖ Saturated Fat: 0.8g
- ❖ Sodium: 320mg

In the vibrant repertoire of the Stuffed Grape Leaves with Rice & Herbs resonate with age-old traditions and tales of shared feasts. Their tender wraps and aromatic fillings transport you to sun-drenched Mediterranean coasts, where each bite is a tribute to heritage and communal joy. As you savor these stuffed leaves, let them remind you of the timeless beauty of simple, heartfelt dishes.

Recipe 77: Roasted Pepper & Walnut Spread

Set the stage for a memorable meal with our Roasted Pepper and walnut Spread, a vibrant appetizer that elegantly combines roasted peppers' smokiness with walnuts' earthiness. While it may sound sophisticated, the beauty of this spread lies in its simplicity. It's a surefire way to impress your guests before the main course arrives. This spread encapsulates the essence of Appetizers to Begin with a Beat, best served with crusty bread or as a dip for fresh vegetables.

Servings: 4-6

Prepping Time: 15 minutes

Cook Time: 10 minutes

Difficulty: Easy

Ingredients:

- 2 large red bell peppers, roasted and peeled
- 1 cup walnuts, toasted
- 2 cloves garlic

- ❖ 2 tbsp olive oil
- ❖ 1 tsp smoked paprika
- ❖ Salt and pepper to taste
- ❖ 1 tbsp lemon juice
- ❖ A handful of chopped parsley

Step-by-Step Preparation:

- ✓ Start by roasting the bell peppers until their skins blister. Once cooled, peel and deseed them.
- ✓ Combine the roasted peppers, walnuts, garlic, olive oil, smoked paprika, and lemon juice in a food processor.
- ✓ Blend until smooth, seasoning with salt and pepper.
- ✓ Transfer the spread to a bowl and garnish with chopped parsley.
- ✓ Chill for at least an hour before serving to let the flavors meld.

Nutritional Facts: (Per serving)

- ❖ Calories: 190
- ❖ Fat: 17g
- ❖ Protein: 4g
- ❖ Carbohydrates: 8g
- ❖ Fiber: 2g
- ❖ Sugars: 4g
- ❖ Sodium: 80mg

The Roasted Pepper and walnut Spread offers a delightful mélange of flavors and a texture, ensuring every bite is an explosion of taste. Its vibrant color and rich consistency make it an appetizer and a visual treat. Given its ease of preparation and minimal ingredients, it's an absolute must-try for those who seek to start their meals on a high note. The combination of roasted peppers and toasted walnuts brings out a familiar and novel taste profile. Whether a dinner party or a simple family meal, this spread will undoubtedly leave a lasting impression, setting the perfect tone for the dishes.

Recipe 78: Tofu Satay with Peanut Sauce

Dive into the rich and flavorsome world of Asian cuisine with our Tofu Satay with Peanut Sauce. This appetizer is a delightful twist on the traditional beef or chicken satay, catering to vegetarians and meat lovers alike. Crispy on the outside and soft within, the tofu skewers transport you to culinary heaven when drizzled with creamy peanut sauce. As part of Appetizers to Begin with a Beat, this dish promises a rhythm of flavors, ensuring every meal starts with a symphonic overture.

Servings: 4

Prepping Time: 20 minutes

Cook Time: 10 minutes

Difficulty: Moderate

Ingredients:

- 1 block of firm tofu, cubed
- 2 tbsp soy sauce
- 1 tbsp sesame oil

- 2 cloves garlic, minced
- 1 cup creamy peanut butter
- 1/2 cup coconut milk
- 1 tbsp lime juice
- 1 tsp chili flakes (adjust to taste)
- 1 tbsp brown sugar
- Wooden skewers soaked in water

Step-by-Step Preparation:

- ✓ Marinate tofu cubes with soy sauce, sesame oil, and minced garlic. Let it sit for 15 minutes.
- ✓ Thread tofu cubes onto soaked wooden skewers.
- ✓ Grill or pan-fry the tofu skewers until golden brown on all sides.
- ✓ Combine peanut butter, coconut milk, lime juice, chili flakes, and brown sugar in a saucepan for the peanut sauce. Cook over medium heat, stirring constantly until smooth.
- ✓ Serve the tofu satay skewers with the warm peanut sauce on the side.

Nutritional Facts: (Per serving)

- Calories: 320
- Fat: 25g
- Protein: 15g
- Carbohydrates: 12g
- Fiber: 3g
- Sugars: 6g
- Sodium: 450mg

Our Tofu Satay with Peanut Sauce is more than just an appetizer; it's an experience. Each skewer encapsulates the beauty of balanced flavors - the umami from tofu, the peanut sauce's richness, and the chili's slight heat. As we explore the symphony of appetizers in this chapter, this dish stands out, presenting comfort and excitement in every bite. It's a testament to the versatility of tofu and the magic of combining simple ingredients to create a dish that resonates with diverse palettes. As you savor this, let it be a reminder that every great meal begins with a powerful intro, and our Tofu Satay does just that.

Recipe 79: Beetroot & Goat Cheese Crostini

Step into a culinary realm where rustic meets refined with our Beetroot and goat Cheese Crostini. A harmonious blend of earthy Beetroot paired with creamy goat cheese, each bite delivers a medley of flavors and textures. Contrasting the rich red of Beetroot with the soft white of the cheese, this appetizer is as visually appealing as it is delicious. As we venture through Appetizers to Begin with a Beat, this dish embodies simple elegance, making every dining occasion feel special.

Servings: 6

Prepping Time: 15 minutes

Cook Time: 10 minutes

Difficulty: Easy

Ingredients:

- 1 medium beetroot, roasted and finely diced
- 150g goat cheese, crumbled
- 1 baguette, sliced into 1/2-inch pieces

- ❖ 2 tbsp olive oil
- ❖ 1 tsp fresh thyme, chopped
- ❖ Salt and pepper to taste
- ❖ Honey for drizzling (optional)

Step-by-Step Preparation:

- ✓ Preheat the oven to 375°F (190°C).
- ✓ Arrange baguette slices on a baking tray and brush with olive oil.
- ✓ Toast in the oven until crisp and golden, about 5 minutes.
- ✓ Mix the roasted Beetroot, thyme, salt, and pepper in a bowl.
- ✓ Once the baguette slices have cooled slightly, top each with a spoonful of beetroot mixture.
- ✓ Crumble goat cheese over the Beetroot.
- ✓ Drizzle with honey if desired, and serve immediately.

Nutritional Facts: (Per serving)

- ❖ Calories: 180
- ❖ Fat: 9g
- ❖ Protein: 6g
- ❖ Carbohydrates: 20g
- ❖ Fiber: 2g
- ❖ Sugars: 4g
- ❖ Sodium: 230mg

The Beetroot & Goat Cheese Crostini is an appetizer that serenades your taste buds with its flavors. As you journey through the array of appetizers in this chapter, this dish stands out, telling a story of how simple ingredients can create gastronomic wonders. Its balance of earthiness, tanginess, and sweetness makes it an irresistible starter that sets the stage for a delectable dining experience. Whether you're hosting a lavish dinner or enjoying a quiet meal with loved ones, this crostini promises to infuse a touch of gourmet elegance into your spread, echoing the essence of "beginning with a beat."

Recipe 80: Chilled Avocado & Cilantro Soup Shots

Savor the sublime fusion of creaminess and zest with our Chilled Avocado and cilantro Soup Shots. This appetizer is a symphony of fresh ingredients, with the lush texture of avocado harmonizing beautifully with the piquant flair of cilantro. Served chilled, each shot glass offers refreshment, making it a perfect palate cleanser or a light start to a hearty meal. Journeying through Appetizers to Begin with a Beat these soup shots stand as a testament to the wonders of culinary creativity, captivating both the eyes and the palate.

Servings: 8

Prepping Time: 15 minutes

Cook Time: No cook time (Chill for 2 hours)

Difficulty: Easy

Ingredients:

- ❖ 2 ripe avocados, peeled and pitted

- ❖ 1 cup vegetable broth
- ❖ 1/2 cup fresh cilantro leaves, chopped
- ❖ 1 tbsp lime juice
- ❖ Salt and pepper to taste
- ❖ 1/2 cup coconut milk
- ❖ Red pepper flakes for garnish (optional)

Step-by-Step Preparation:

- ✓ Combine avocados, vegetable broth, cilantro, lime juice, salt, and pepper in a blender.
- ✓ Blend until smooth, adding coconut milk to achieve desired consistency.
- ✓ Taste and adjust seasoning if needed.
- ✓ Pour the mixture into shot glasses or small cups.
- ✓ Chill in the refrigerator for at least 2 hours.
- ✓ Before serving, garnish with a sprinkle of red pepper flakes if desired.

Nutritional Facts: (Per serving)

- ❖ Calories: 110
- ❖ Fat: 9g
- ❖ Protein: 1g
- ❖ Carbohydrates: 8g
- ❖ Fiber: 4g
- ❖ Sugars: 1g
- ❖ Sodium: 120mg

The Chilled Avocado and cilantro Soup Shots elegantly encapsulate the essence of sophisticated simplicity. This appetizer, while easy to prepare, offers a dance of flavors that is both refreshing and indulgent. Each sip promises a velvety texture juxtaposed with the spirited kick of cilantro and lime, ensuring a memorable start to any meal. As we traverse the realm of appetizers in this chapter, these soup shots emerge as a beacon of culinary innovation, proving that sometimes the most delightful experiences come in small packages. Ideal for summer soirées or chic dinner parties, this dish reminds us that every culinary journey, no matter how grand, starts with a single, delectable beat.

Chapter 09: Crunchy, Fresh Salads for a Strong Heart

Recipe 81: Green Goddess Kale & Avocado Salad

Indulge in a culinary embrace of nature's finest with our Green Goddess Kale & Avocado Salad. This refreshing ensemble celebrates the vibrancy of green, intertwining the wholesome goodness of kale with the creamy delight of avocado. Infused with a dressing that sings of herbs and citrus, every forkful is an invigorating dance of flavors and textures. As we venture into Crunchy, Fresh Salads for a Strong Heart, this dish stands out, championing heart health without compromising taste or elegance.

Servings: 4

Prepping Time: 20 minutes

Cook Time: No cook time

Difficulty: Easy

Ingredients:

- ❖ 4 cups kale, stemmed and torn into bite-sized pieces
- ❖ 2 ripe avocados, diced
- ❖ 1/2 cup chopped parsley
- ❖ 1/4 cup chopped tarragon
- ❖ 1/4 cup chives, finely chopped
- ❖ 1 lemon, juiced
- ❖ 2 tbsp olive oil
- ❖ Salt and pepper to taste
- ❖ 1/4 cup toasted pine nuts

Step-by-Step Preparation:

- ✓ Massage the kale with a pinch of salt in a large bowl until it softens and turns a brighter green.
- ✓ Add diced avocados to the bowl.
- ✓ Whisk together parsley, tarragon, chives, lemon juice, olive oil, salt, and pepper in a separate small bowl to make the dressing.
- ✓ Drizzle the dressing over the kale and avocado, tossing gently to combine.
- ✓ Garnish with toasted pine nuts.
- ✓ Serve immediately.

Nutritional Facts: (Per serving)

- ❖ Calories: 280
- ❖ Fat: 23g
- ❖ Protein: 6g
- ❖ Carbohydrates: 20g
- ❖ Fiber: 8g
- ❖ Sugars: 2g
- ❖ Sodium: 80mg

The Green Goddess Kale & Avocado Salad is a testament to the beauty of nature's bounty, showcasing how health and indulgence can coexist harmoniously on a plate. As we explore the landscape of crunchy, fresh salads in this chapter, this offering captivates us with its rich medley of flavors, promising nourishment for both the body and soul. It's not just a salad; it's an experience - a melody of crisp kale, creamy avocado, and zesty dressing, all crowned with the gentle crunch of pine nuts.

Recipe 82: Roasted Beet & Arugula with Walnuts

Indulge in the heart-healthy wonders of "Roasted Beet & Arugula with Walnuts" beef stir fry. A fusion of earthy beets, zesty arugula, crunchy walnuts, and savory beef brings a powerhouse of nutrients. This tantalizing recipe is a perfect blend of flavors, marrying the freshness of a salad with the robustness of a beef stir fry. Dive into this culinary experience that ensures every bite not only tantalizes your taste buds but also provides numerous benefits for a strong heart.

Servings: 4

Prepping Time: 20 minutes

Cook Time: 15 minutes

Difficulty: Moderate

Ingredients:

- ❖ 2 medium-sized beets, peeled and diced
- ❖ 200g of lean beef strips

- ❖ 2 cups of arugula
- ❖ 1/2 cup of walnuts, chopped
- ❖ 2 tbsp olive oil
- ❖ 2 garlic cloves, minced
- ❖ Salt and pepper, to taste
- ❖ 2 tbsp balsamic vinegar

Step-by-Step Preparation:

- ✓ Preheat oven to 400°F (200°C).
- ✓ Toss beets in 1 tbsp olive oil, salt, and pepper. Spread on a baking sheet and roast for 20 minutes or until tender.
- ✓ In a pan, heat the remaining olive oil over medium heat. Add garlic and sauté until fragrant.
- ✓ Add beef strips to the pan, cooking until browned on all sides.
- ✓ Combine roasted beets, arugula, beef, and walnuts in a large bowl.
- ✓ Drizzle with balsamic vinegar, toss well, and serve immediately.

Nutritional Facts: (Per serving)

- ❖ Calories: 250
- ❖ Protein: 18g
- ❖ Fat: 16g
- ❖ Carbohydrates: 10g
- ❖ Dietary Fiber: 3g
- ❖ Sugars: 6g
- ❖ Sodium: 80mg

Finding the perfect balance between health and flavor can often be challenging, but this "Roasted Beet & Arugula with Walnuts" beef stir fry epitomizes that sweet spot. The deep hues of the beets, contrasted with the verdant greens of arugula and highlighted by the rich taste of beef, ensure a visually delightful plate. More importantly, every ingredient has been carefully chosen to boost heart health. Adding walnuts not only elevates the texture but also brings many benefits, from omega-3 fatty acids to antioxidant properties. So, the next time you seek a delightful and nourishing meal, remember this heart-healthy symphony on a plate.

Recipe 83: Lively Lemon Quinoa Salad

Welcome a burst of zesty freshness with our Lively Lemon Quinoa Salad. Infused with the refreshing tang of lemon, this dish beautifully showcases quinoa, a grain known for its high nutritional content and versatility. Paired with vibrant vegetables, this salad embodies rejuvenation in every spoonful. As we celebrate Crunchy, Fresh Salads for a Strong Heart, this salad is a testament to the joy of wholesome eating, promising both nourishment and an irresistible treat for the taste buds.

Servings: 4

Prepping Time: 20 minutes

Cook Time: 15 minutes

Difficulty: Easy

Ingredients:

- 1 cup quinoa, rinsed and drained
- 2 cups water
- Zest and juice of 1 lemon

- ❖ 1 cucumber, diced
- ❖ 1 red bell pepper, diced
- ❖ 1/4 cup fresh parsley, finely chopped
- ❖ 1/4 cup olive oil
- ❖ Salt and pepper to taste
- ❖ 1/4 cup crumbled feta cheese (optional)

Step-by-Step Preparation:

- ✓ In a saucepan, combine quinoa and water. Bring to a boil, reduce heat, cover, and simmer for 15 minutes or until quinoa is tender.
- ✓ Fluff quinoa with a fork and let it cool.
- ✓ Combine the cooled quinoa, cucumber, bell pepper, and parsley in a large mixing bowl.
- ✓ Whisk together lemon zest, lemon juice, olive oil, salt, and pepper in a separate bowl to create the dressing.
- ✓ Pour the dressing over the quinoa mixture and toss to combine.
- ✓ Garnish with feta cheese if desired.
- ✓ Chill before serving.

Nutritional Facts: (Per serving)

- ❖ Calories: 260
- ❖ Fat: 12g
- ❖ Protein: 7g
- ❖ Carbohydrates: 32g
- ❖ Fiber: 4g
- ❖ Sugars: 3g
- ❖ Sodium: 180mg

The Lively Lemon Quinoa Salad is a beacon of fresh, heart-healthy eating. As we journey through this chapter dedicated to crunchy, vibrant salads, this dish stands as a perfect embodiment of taste and nutrition intertwined. The light, citrusy undertones of the salad are complemented by the rich textures of quinoa and veggies, making it a delightful experience for the palate. Beyond its flavor, this salad is a powerhouse of nutrients, underscoring that eating well can be delightful and nourishing. Whether you're hosting a brunch, a picnic, or simply seeking a refreshing meal, this salad promises to be a favorite, affirming that every heartbeat echoes the goodness of what we feed it.

Recipe 84: Summer Corn & Tomato Salad

Celebrate summer's bounty with the vibrant and refreshing Summer Corn and Tomato Salad. This dish captures the essence of sun-kissed days and balmy nights, merging the sweetness of fresh corn with the tangy burst of ripe tomatoes. Each bite is a dance of flavors and textures, evoking memories of picnics and al fresco dining. As we turn the pages of Crunchy, Fresh Salads for a Strong Heart, this salad is a radiant emblem of seasonal freshness, weaving health and hedonism in a delightful culinary tapestry.

Servings: 4

Prepping Time: 15 minutes

Cook Time: No cook time

Difficulty: Easy

Ingredients:

- 3 ears of fresh corn, kernels removed
- 2 cups cherry tomatoes, halved
- 1/4 cup fresh basil, chopped
- 2 tbsp olive oil

- 1 tbsp apple cider vinegar
- Salt and pepper to taste
- 1/4 cup crumbled feta cheese (optional)

Step-by-Step Preparation:

- ✓ In a large mixing bowl, combine corn kernels and halved cherry tomatoes.
- ✓ Whisk together olive oil, apple cider vinegar, salt, and pepper in a separate small bowl to create the dressing.
- ✓ Pour the dressing over the corn and tomato mixture.
- ✓ Add chopped basil and toss gently to combine all ingredients.
- ✓ If desired, sprinkle with crumbled feta cheese for an added layer of flavor.
- ✓ Chill for 30 minutes before serving to let the flavors meld.

Nutritional Facts: (Per serving)

- Calories: 160
- Fat: 9g
- Protein: 4g
- Carbohydrates: 18g
- Fiber: 2g
- Sugars: 5g
- Sodium: 100mg

The Summer Corn & Tomato Salad is a melodic ode to the season's best offerings, harmoniously merging taste and nutrition. As we explore salads that champion heart health in this chapter, this dish shines brightly, a reminder of how nature's simplest ingredients can come together in a symphony of flavors. The blend of sweet corn, tangy tomatoes, and aromatic basil is reminiscent of summer's joyful embrace, ensuring every meal feels like a sunlit celebration. Perfect for gatherings, picnics, or as a refreshing side, this salad embodies the spirit of summer, promising a heart-healthy journey that is as delightful as a sun-soaked day.

Recipe 85: Heart-Healthy Greek Salad

A mosaic of vibrant colors and flavors, this salad combines crisp vegetables with tangy olives and creamy feta, epitomizing the essence of Greek culinary traditions. Each bite is a testament to the balance of freshness and richness, making it a timeless favorite for many. As we explore Crunchy, Fresh Salads for a Strong Heart, this dish stands as a celebration of heart-healthy ingredients, presenting both culinary delight and nutritional benefits.

Servings: 4

Prepping Time: 20 minutes

Cook Time: No cook time

Difficulty: Easy

Ingredients:

- 3 medium tomatoes, chopped
- 1 cucumber, diced
- 1 red onion, thinly sliced
- 1/2 cup Kalamata olives

- ❖ 1/2 cup feta cheese, crumbled
- ❖ 2 tbsp olive oil
- ❖ 1 tbsp red wine vinegar
- ❖ 1 tsp dried oregano
- ❖ Salt and pepper to taste
- ❖ A handful of fresh parsley, chopped

Step-by-Step Preparation:

- ✓ Combine tomatoes, cucumber, red onion, and Kalamata olives in a large mixing bowl.
- ✓ Whisk together olive oil, red wine vinegar, oregano, salt, and pepper in a separate small bowl to create the dressing.
- ✓ Drizzle the dressing over the vegetable mixture.
- ✓ Gently toss the salad to ensure all ingredients are well-coated.
- ✓ Top with crumbled feta cheese and a sprinkle of fresh parsley.
- ✓ Chill for at least 30 minutes before serving to enhance the flavors.

Nutritional Facts: (Per serving)

- ❖ Calories: 180
- ❖ Fat: 12g
- ❖ Protein: 5g
- ❖ Carbohydrates: 14g
- ❖ Fiber: 3g
- ❖ Sugars: 7g
- ❖ Sodium: 330mg

The Heart-Healthy Greek Salad is not just a dish but an experience. This offering beautifully blends health and taste as we delve into salads designed to keep our hearts in prime condition. It's a tribute to the Mediterranean diet, renowned for its cardiovascular benefits. The harmonious balance of crisp veggies, salty olives, and creamy feta evokes memories of sea breeze and sun-drenched terraces. Ideal for a light lunch, a side dish, or a part of a grand feast, this salad encapsulates the joy of eating well. Every bite is a reminder that heart health can be as delightful and vibrant as a Grecian sunset.

Recipe 86: Rainbow Carrot & Radish Slaw

Venture into a vivid world of colors and flavors with our Rainbow Carrot & Radish Slaw. This salad is a canvas of radiant hues, intertwining the playful shades of rainbow carrots with the boldness of radishes. It's a delightful mingling of crisp textures and subtle flavors, promising a refreshing bite every time. As we progress through Crunchy, Fresh Salads for a Strong Heart, this slaw emerges as a visual and gustatory delight, symbolizing the joy of eating fresh, wholesome ingredients.

Servings: 4

Prepping Time: 15 minutes

Cook Time: No cook time

Difficulty: Easy

Ingredients:

- ❖ 4 rainbow carrots, julienned or grated

- 6 radishes, thinly sliced
- 1/4 cup fresh cilantro, chopped
- 3 tbsp olive oil
- 2 tbsp apple cider vinegar
- 1 tsp honey or maple syrup
- Salt and pepper to taste
- 1 tbsp sesame seeds, toasted (optional)

Step-by-Step Preparation:

- ✓ Combine julienned carrots, sliced radishes, and chopped cilantro in a large mixing bowl.
- ✓ Whisk together olive oil, apple cider vinegar, honey or maple syrup, salt, and pepper in a separate bowl to craft the dressing.
- ✓ Pour the dressing over the carrot and radish mixture, tossing gently to combine.
- ✓ If desired, sprinkle with toasted sesame seeds for a crunch and flavor.
- ✓ Chill for about 30 minutes before serving to let the flavors meld.

Nutritional Facts: (Per serving)

- Calories: 110
- Fat: 9g
- Protein: 1g
- Carbohydrates: 8g
- Fiber: 2g
- Sugars: 4g
- Sodium: 80mg

The Rainbow Carrot & Radish Slaw is a vibrant ode to nature's color palette, bringing joy to the plate and palate alike. As we traverse the realm of heart-healthy salads in this chapter, this slaw stands as a testament to the beauty of simplicity. The harmonious blend of crunchy textures and a delicate dressing creates a dance of flavors that's both invigorating and soothing. It's an ideal companion for picnics, BBQs or as a bright side to any main dish. With every colorful forkful, this salad reminds us that heart health can be celebrated with a medley of hues and that every bite can be a vibrant journey for the senses.

Recipe 87: Spinach, Orange, & Almond Delight

Experience a refreshing symphony of flavors with our Spinach, Orange, and almond Delight. This salad seamlessly melds the tender leaves of spinach with the citrusy zing of fresh oranges, all punctuated by the crunch of toasted almonds. It's a culinary canvas of textures and tastes, ensuring each bite are refreshing and satisfying. As we delve deeper into Crunchy, Fresh Salads for a Strong Heart, this delightful ensemble is a testament to the harmonious blend of nature's offerings, providing pleasure and heart health in a single dish.

Servings: 4

Prepping Time: 20 minutes

Cook Time: No cook time

Difficulty: Easy

Ingredients:

- ❖ 4 cups fresh spinach, washed and torn
- ❖ 2 large oranges, peeled and segmented

- 1/2 cup almonds, toasted and roughly chopped
- 2 tbsp olive oil
- 1 tbsp fresh orange juice
- 1 tsp honey
- Salt and pepper to taste
- Zest of 1 orange

Step-by-Step Preparation:

- In a large bowl, combine spinach leaves and orange segments.
- Whisk together olive oil, fresh orange juice, honey, orange zest, salt, and pepper in a small bowl to create a zesty dressing.
- Pour the dressing over the spinach and orange mixture, ensuring everything is well-coated.
- Sprinkle with toasted almonds for a crunchy finish.
- Serve immediately for the freshest taste.

Nutritional Facts: (Per serving)

- Calories: 180
- Fat: 12g
- Protein: 5g
- Carbohydrates: 16g
- Fiber: 4g
- Sugars: 10g
- Sodium: 60mg

The Spinach, Orange, and almond Delight is not just a salad; it's a vibrant embrace of freshness and flavor. As we traverse the pathways of heart-healthy salads in this chapter, this dish shines brightly, epitomizing the idea that nutrition and gourmet dining can go hand in hand. The medley of tender spinach, zesty oranges, and crunchy almonds portrays culinary perfection, promising to invigorate the heart and soul. Whether it's a summer soirée or a quiet evening meal, this salad is a fitting tribute to the joys of fresh produce and the rhythm of a strong heart, ensuring every meal resonates with the melody of well-being.

Recipe 88: Crispy Tofu & Broccoli Salad

Indulge in a fusion of flavors and textures with our Crispy Tofu and broccoli Salad. This dish elegantly pairs the crunch of golden-brown tofu with the vibrant green and tender bite of lightly steamed broccoli. Drizzled with a savory dressing, this salad is a delightful mingling of health and taste, promising satisfaction with every forkful. As we navigate Crunchy, Fresh Salads for a Strong Heart, this ensemble shines as an example of culinary artistry, highlighting the beauty of plant-based ingredients.

Servings: 4

Prepping Time: 25 minutes

Cook Time: 20 minutes

Difficulty: Moderate

Ingredients:

- 1 block of firm tofu, cubed and pressed
- 4 cups broccoli florets
- 3 tbsp sesame oil

- 2 tbsp soy sauce
- 1 tbsp rice vinegar
- 1 tsp ginger, minced
- 2 garlic cloves, minced
- 1 tbsp sesame seeds
- Salt and pepper to taste

Step-by-Step Preparation:

- ✓ Heat 2 tablespoons of sesame oil in a skillet over medium heat.
- ✓ Add tofu cubes and fry until golden and crispy on all sides.
- ✓ Blanch broccoli florets in a pot of boiling water for 2-3 minutes. Drain and set aside.
- ✓ Whisk together soy sauce, rice vinegar, 1 tablespoon of sesame oil, ginger, and garlic for the dressing.
- ✓ In a large bowl, combine crispy tofu and blanched broccoli.
- ✓ Drizzle with the prepared dressing and toss to coat evenly.
- ✓ Garnish with sesame seeds and serve.

Nutritional Facts: (Per serving)

- Calories: 210
- Fat: 14g
- Protein: 12g
- Carbohydrates: 13g
- Fiber: 4g
- Sugars: 2g
- Sodium: 450mg

The Crispy Tofu & Broccoli Salad embodies culinary harmony, a dance of flavors and textures that celebrates the essence of fresh, heart-healthy ingredients. As we delve into salads crafted for a strong heart in this chapter, this dish stands out, showcasing how simple ingredients can be transformed into a gourmet delight. The juxtaposition of crispy tofu and tender broccoli, combined with the aromatic dressing, promises a nourishing and indulgent experience. Perfect for a hearty lunch or a refreshing side, this salad is a testament to the idea that eating for heart health can be a flavorful and fulfilling journey, one bite at a time.

Recipe 89: Mediterranean Bulgar & Chickpea Salad

Embark on a culinary journey to sun-soaked shores with our Mediterranean Bulgar & Chickpea Salad. Infused with the vibrant flavors of the Mediterranean, this dish combines bulgur's nutty goodness with chickpea's hearty texture, all harmoniously blended with fresh herbs and a zesty dressing. It's a salad that radiates warmth and wellness, echoing the traditional diets of those who live by the Mediterranean Sea. As we immerse ourselves in Crunchy, Fresh Salads for a Strong Heart, this ensemble embodies a timeless tradition of combining taste with heart-healthy benefits.

Servings: 4

Prepping Time: 20 minutes

Cook Time: 15 minutes

Difficulty: Moderate

Ingredients:

- 1 cup bulgar

- 2 cups water
- 1 can chickpeas, drained and rinsed
- 1/2 cup fresh parsley, finely chopped
- 1/2 cup fresh mint, finely chopped
- 1/4 cup olive oil
- Juice of 1 lemon
- 1 garlic clove, minced
- Salt and pepper to taste
- 1/2 cup cherry tomatoes, halved
- 1/4 cup feta cheese, crumbled (optional)

Step-by-Step Preparation:

- In a saucepan, bring water to a boil. Add bulgar, reduce heat, cover, and simmer for about 15 minutes or until tender.
- Fluff bulgar with a fork and transfer to a large mixing bowl to cool.
- Add chickpeas, parsley, mint, and cherry tomatoes to the cooled bulgar.
- Whisk together olive oil, lemon juice, garlic, salt, and pepper in a separate bowl to create the dressing.
- Pour the dressing over the bulgar mixture and toss to combine.
- If desired, sprinkle with crumbled feta cheese.
- Chill for about 30 minutes before serving for the flavors to meld.

Nutritional Facts: (Per serving)

- Calories: 290
- Fat: 12g
- Protein: 9g
- Carbohydrates: 38g
- Fiber: 9g
- Sugars: 3g
- Sodium: 220mg

The Mediterranean Bulgar & Chickpea Salad is a sensory voyage to azure waters and sunlit terrains, bringing the essence of Mediterranean dining to your plate. As we continue our exploration of heart-healthy salads in this chapter, this dish stands tall, embodying a rich heritage of taste and nutrition. It's a celebration of simple ingredients coming together in a delightful dance of flavors, promising pleasure and health in every bite.

Recipe 90: Fresh Herb & Mixed Greens Salad

Dive into a verdant oasis of flavor with our Fresh Herb and mixed Greens Salad. This dish is a tribute to nature's finest green offerings, blending fresh herbs with a medley of mixed greens. It's a refreshing ensemble, vibrant in taste and appearance, and captures the very essence of a garden on a plate. As we savor our way through Crunchy, Fresh Salads for a Strong Heart, this salad emerges as a quintessential choice, championing freshness, simplicity, and heart-healthy goodness.

Servings: 4

Prepping Time: 20 minutes

Cook Time: No cook time

Difficulty: Easy

Ingredients:

- 4 cups mixed salad greens (like arugula, spinach, and romaine)
- 1/2 cup fresh basil leaves
- 1/4 cup fresh mint leaves

- ❖ 1/4 cup fresh cilantro leaves
- ❖ 2 tbsp olive oil
- ❖ 1 tbsp lemon juice
- ❖ Salt and pepper to taste
- ❖ 1/4 cup toasted pine nuts

Step-by-Step Preparation:

- ✓ In a large salad bowl, combine mixed greens and fresh herbs.
- ✓ Whisk together olive oil, lemon juice, salt, and pepper in a separate small bowl to create a light dressing.
- ✓ Drizzle the dressing over the greens and herbs, tossing gently to coat.
- ✓ Garnish with toasted pine nuts for added crunch.
- ✓ Serve immediately for peak freshness.

Nutritional Facts: (Per serving)

- ❖ Calories: 120
- ❖ Fat: 10g
- ❖ Protein: 3g
- ❖ Carbohydrates: 6g
- ❖ Fiber: 2g
- ❖ Sugars: 1g
- ❖ Sodium: 50mg

The Fresh Herb & Mixed Greens Salad celebrates nature's bounty, a testament to the beauty of fresh, uncomplicated ingredients. As we venture through heart-healthy salads in this chapter, this offering stands out as a beacon of freshness and vitality. It invites you to experience the essence of a thriving garden, where each bite resonates with crispness and aromatic allure. Perfect for sunny brunches or as an uplifting side to any main dish, this salad underscores the joy of wholesome eating. Embracing heart health has never been more delightful, ensuring every meal becomes an ode to nature's unparalleled generosity.

Chapter 10: Party Plates: Celebrate the Low-Cholesterol Way

Recipe 91: Mini Veggie & Hummus Cups

Dazzle your guests with a clever twist on veggie dipping—our Mini Veggie & Hummus Cups. These delightful bites transform the usual platter setup into individual, elegant servings, ensuring a balanced scoop of hummus with every veggie stick. Perfect for cocktail hours, picnics, or any gathering, these cups are a nod to health and sophistication. As we embark on Party Plates: Celebrate the Low-Cholesterol Way, these veggie cups are the epitome of festive yet health-conscious fare.

Servings: 6

Prepping Time: 20 minutes

Cook Time: No cook time

Difficulty: Easy

Ingredients:

- 1 cup hummus, store-bought or homemade
- 2 carrots, peeled and cut into thin sticks
- 2 cucumbers, cut into thin sticks
- 1 bell pepper, sliced into thin strips
- 6 small glasses or clear cups
- Fresh parsley or cilantro for garnish

Step-by-Step Preparation:

- ✓ Place a generous dollop of hummus at the base of each glass or cup.
- ✓ Arrange an assortment of carrot, cucumber, and bell pepper sticks vertically into the hummus, ensuring each cup has a colorful mix.
- ✓ Garnish with a sprig of parsley or cilantro.
- ✓ Chill until ready to serve.

Nutritional Facts: (Per serving)

- Calories: 90
- Fat: 5g
- Protein: 3g
- Carbohydrates: 9g
- Fiber: 3g
- Sugars: 2g
- Sodium: 130mg

The Mini Veggie & Hummus Cups are more than just a delightful appetizer; they're a statement. As we navigate this chapter dedicated to low-cholesterol party treats, these cups are a testament to creativity and health coexisting harmoniously. They embody the joy of celebration while championing intelligent, heart-healthy choices. Whether a grand festivity or an intimate gathering, these veggie cups ensure every celebration is stylish and wholesome. With each bite, guests are reminded that festive feasting can be heart-friendly, turning every occasion into a celebration of well-being.

Recipe 92: Olive Tapenade & Whole Wheat Crackers

Elevate your party platters with the rich, Mediterranean flavors of our Olive Tapenade and Whole Wheat Crackers. This classic spread, made from a medley of olives, capers, and herbs, pairs perfectly with the wholesome crunch of whole wheat crackers. It's a pairing that boasts flavor and heart health, proving that celebratory treats can be indulgent and nourishing. As we unveil Party Plates: Celebrate the Low-Cholesterol Way, this tapenade emerges as a quintessential choice for those looking to balance festivities with thoughtful nutrition.

Servings: 6-8

Prepping Time: 15 minutes

Cook Time: No cook time

Difficulty: Easy

Ingredients:

- 1 cup mixed olives (pitted)

- ❖ 2 tbsp capers
- ❖ 1 garlic clove
- ❖ 2 tbsp olive oil
- ❖ 1 tsp lemon zest
- ❖ Juice of 1 lemon
- ❖ 1/4 cup fresh parsley
- ❖ Whole wheat crackers for serving

Step-by-Step Preparation:

- ✓ Combine olives, capers, garlic, olive oil, lemon zest, lemon juice, and parsley in a food processor.
- ✓ Pulse until the mixture is coarsely chopped and well-blended.
- ✓ Transfer the tapenade to a serving bowl.
- ✓ Arrange whole wheat crackers around the bowl or serve separately.
- ✓ Garnish with an extra drizzle of olive oil or a sprig of parsley if desired.

Nutritional Facts: (Per serving)

- ❖ Calories: 70
- ❖ Fat: 6g
- ❖ Protein: 1g
- ❖ Carbohydrates: 4g
- ❖ Fiber: 1g
- ❖ Sugars: 0g
- ❖ Sodium: 180mg

The Olive Tapenade & Whole Wheat Crackers pairing is a timeless treat that effortlessly blends gourmet flavors with health-conscious choices. As we celebrate with low-cholesterol party plates in this chapter, this ensemble stands out, showcasing how age-old recipes can be tailored to modern health needs. Each bite is a delightful fusion of the salty Mediterranean with the wholesome crunch of whole grains, turning any gathering into a sophisticated affair. It's a reminder that celebrations can be both luxurious and heart-friendly, ensuring every festivity resonates with the warmth of good health and the joy of great taste.

Recipe 93: Baked Spinach & Artichoke Dip

Infuse your party with warmth and flavor by introducing the ever-popular Baked Spinach and artichoke Dip. This creamy concoction combines the tender goodness of spinach and the unique texture of artichokes, enveloped in a velvety mix and baked to golden perfection. It's comfort food that appeals to the senses and adheres to heart-healthy standards. As we journey through Party Plates: Celebrate the Low-Cholesterol Way, this dip exemplifies how classic favorites can be artfully reimagined to prioritize health without compromising taste.

Servings: 6-8

Prepping Time: 15 minutes

Cook Time: 25 minutes

Difficulty: Moderate

Ingredients:

- 1 cup fresh spinach, chopped
- 1 can (14 oz) artichoke hearts, drained and chopped

- ❖ 1/2 cup low-fat cream cheese
- ❖ 1/4 cup Greek yogurt
- ❖ 1/4 cup grated Parmesan cheese
- ❖ 2 garlic cloves, minced
- ❖ Salt and pepper to taste
- ❖ 1/4 cup shredded mozzarella cheese

Step-by-Step Preparation:

- ✓ Preheat oven to 375°F (190°C).
- ✓ Mix spinach, artichoke hearts, cream cheese, Greek yogurt, Parmesan cheese, garlic, salt, and pepper in a mixing bowl. Mix until well combined.
- ✓ Transfer the mixture to a baking dish, spreading it out evenly.
- ✓ Sprinkle shredded mozzarella cheese on top.
- ✓ Bake in the oven for 20-25 minutes or until the top is golden brown and bubbly.
- ✓ Serve warm with whole grain crackers, vegetable sticks, or toasted bread.

Nutritional Facts: (Per serving)

- ❖ Calories: 130
- ❖ Fat: 7g
- ❖ Protein: 6g
- ❖ Carbohydrates: 10g
- ❖ Fiber: 3g
- ❖ Sugars: 2g
- ❖ Sodium: 250mg

The Baked Spinach and Artichoke Dip is not just a dish but an experience – a warm embrace in a bowl, bringing together friends and family. As we navigate this chapter of low-cholesterol party delights, this dip stands as a beacon of the notion that indulgence and health coexist in perfect harmony. Every scoop reminds one of the pleasures of hearty flavors and the satisfaction of making heart-friendly choices. Whether it's a holiday gathering, a weekend game night, or a cozy evening, this dip ensures the spotlight shines brightly on taste and health, making every celebration heartwarming.

Recipe 94: Heart-Friendly Mini Pizzas

Revel in the joy of bite-sized delights with our Heart-Friendly Mini Pizzas. These petite wonders encapsulate all the flavors of a classic pizza but with ingredients carefully chosen to be kinder to the heart. Crafted with whole grain crusts and topped with fresh, low-cholesterol toppings, these mini pizzas are perfect for satisfying cravings without guilt. As we dive into Party Plates: Celebrate the Low-Cholesterol Way, these miniatures champion the idea that favorite comfort foods can be delicious and heart-conscious.

Servings: 8

Prepping Time: 20 minutes

Cook Time: 12 minutes

Difficulty: Moderate

Ingredients:

- 8 whole grain mini pizza crusts
- 1/2 cup low-sodium tomato sauce
- 1 cup shredded mozzarella (part-skim)
- 1/2 cup bell peppers, finely diced

- 1/2 cup cherry tomatoes, halved
- 1/4 cup fresh basil leaves
- 2 garlic cloves, minced
- Olive oil for brushing
- Salt and pepper to taste

Step-by-Step Preparation:

- Preheat oven to 425°F (220°C).
- Arrange mini pizza crusts on a baking tray.
- Brush a thin layer of olive oil over each crust.
- Evenly spread the tomato sauce over each crust, leaving a small border.
- Sprinkle the shredded mozzarella, followed by bell peppers and cherry tomatoes.
- Add a dash of minced garlic to each mini pizza.
- Season with salt and pepper to taste.
- Bake in the oven for 10-12 minutes or until the crust is golden and the cheese is bubbly.
- Garnish with fresh basil leaves before serving.

Nutritional Facts: (Per serving)

- Calories: 140
- Fat: 5g
- Protein: 6g
- Carbohydrates: 18g
- Fiber: 3g
- Sugars: 2g
- Sodium: 190mg

Heart-Friendly Mini Pizzas are more than just a treat; they celebrate the balance between indulgence and health. As we traverse the realm of low-cholesterol party offerings in this chapter, these mini pizzas shine brightly, showcasing that traditional favorites can be reinvented with a heart-healthy twist. Whether it's a casual get-together or a more formal soiree, these miniatures promise to be a crowd-pleaser, ensuring that every bite is a testament to the joys of thoughtful, delicious eating.

Recipe 95: Grilled Asparagus with Lemon Zest

Elevate your party spread with the simple elegance of Grilled Asparagus with Lemon Zest. This dish showcases the natural, earthy flavors of asparagus, enhanced by a hint of smokiness from grilling and the refreshing zing of lemon zest. A side that's visually appealing and brimming with nutrients, it's the perfect accompaniment to any main dish or even as a standalone star. As we continue our culinary voyage in Party Plates: Celebrate the Low-Cholesterol Way, this grilled delight reinforces the belief that elegant food can be effortlessly achieved while prioritizing heart health.

Servings: 4

Prepping Time: 10 minutes

Cook Time: 15 minutes

Difficulty: Easy

Ingredients:

- 1 lb fresh asparagus spears, trimmed
- 2 tbsp olive oil

- ❖ Zest of 1 lemon
- ❖ Salt and pepper to taste
- ❖ Lemon wedges for serving

Step-by-Step Preparation:

- ✓ Preheat the grill to medium-high heat.
- ✓ In a mixing bowl, toss asparagus spears with olive oil, ensuring they are evenly coated.
- ✓ Season with salt and pepper.
- ✓ Place asparagus on the grill, turning occasionally, for about 12-15 minutes or until tender and slightly charred.
- ✓ Transfer grilled asparagus to a serving platter.
- ✓ Sprinkle with lemon zest.
- ✓ Serve with lemon wedges on the side.

Nutritional Facts: (Per serving)

- ❖ Calories: 90
- ❖ Fat: 7g
- ❖ Protein: 3g
- ❖ Carbohydrates: 6g
- ❖ Fiber: 3g
- ❖ Sugars: 2g
- ❖ Sodium: 2mg

Grilled Asparagus with Lemon Zest is more than just a side; it's an ode to nature's simplicity. As we explore heart-healthy party dishes in this chapter, this dish shines with its minimalist approach, letting the quality ingredients speak for themselves. The harmonious blend of smoky grill flavors with the aromatic zest of lemon encapsulates celebration and health. Ideal for al fresco dinners, family barbecues, or elegant soirées, this dish assures that heart health can seamlessly meld with gourmet dining. Every bite is a reminder of nature's bountiful offerings, celebrating life, health, and the joys of shared meals.

Recipe 96: Mixed Berry & Chia Seed Pudding Cups

Dive into a delightful fusion of taste and texture with our Mixed Berry and chia Seed Pudding Cups. A delectable blend of creamy chia pudding and vibrant, juicy berries offers a symphony of flavors that dance on the palate. These pudding cups are a visual treat and a reservoir of nutrients, ensuring indulgence aligns with wellness. As we navigate the vibrant lanes of Party Plates: Celebrate the Low-Cholesterol Way, these pudding cups present a delightful intersection of celebration, taste, and heart-healthy choices.

Servings: 6

Prepping Time: 15 minutes (plus several hours for soaking)

Cook Time: No cook time

Difficulty: Easy

Ingredients:

- ❖ 1/4 cup chia seeds
- ❖ 2 cups almond milk (or any preferred milk)

- ❖ 1 tsp vanilla extract
- ❖ 2 tbsp maple syrup or honey
- ❖ 1 cup mixed berries (like strawberries, blueberries, and raspberries)
- ❖ Mint leaves for garnish

Step-by-Step Preparation:

- ✓ Combine chia seeds, almond milk, vanilla extract, and maple syrup in a mixing bowl.
- ✓ Stir well and let the mixture sit for about 10 minutes. Stir again to prevent clumping.
- ✓ Cover the bowl and refrigerate for several hours or overnight, allowing the chia seeds to expand and form a pudding-like consistency.
- ✓ Once set, give the pudding a good stir. If it's too thick, add more almond milk to reach the desired consistency.
- ✓ Spoon the chia pudding into individual cups or glasses.
- ✓ Top with a generous helping of mixed berries.
- ✓ Garnish with mint leaves before serving.

Nutritional Facts: (Per serving)

- ❖ Calories: 120
- ❖ Fat: 4g
- ❖ Protein: 3g
- ❖ Carbohydrates: 18g
- ❖ Fiber: 6g
- ❖ Sugars: 9g
- ❖ Sodium: 60mg

The Mixed Berry & Chia Seed Pudding Cups embody celebration in a cup, blending aesthetics with nutrition. As we journey through low-cholesterol party plates in this chapter, these cups stand out as an emblem of modern gourmet trends, emphasizing the beauty of natural, heart-healthy ingredients. Whether served at brunches, evening soirées, or intimate gatherings, these pudding cups ensure a moment of pause, an indulgent respite, and a shared joy of mindful eating. They highlight that party foods can be tantalizing to the taste buds and a toast to good health, turning every occasion into a well-being festival.

Recipe 97: Pesto & Sun-Dried Tomato Pinwheels

Unfurl layers of flavors with the Pesto and sun-dried Tomato Pinwheels—a perfect bite-sized treat for any festive occasion. These delightful spirals boast vibrant colors and flavors, harmoniously marrying the aromatic punch of Pesto with the concentrated essence of sun-dried tomatoes. As a visually enticing and palate-pleasing appetizer, they exemplify the sophisticated side of healthy eating. Navigating through Party Plates: Celebrate the Low-Cholesterol Way; these pinwheels are a testament to the art of blending tradition, innovation, and wellness.

Servings: 8

Prepping Time: 15 minutes

Cook Time: No cook time

Difficulty: Easy

Ingredients:

- ❖ 2 large whole wheat tortillas

- ❖ 1/2 cup basil pesto
- ❖ 1/2 cup sun-dried tomatoes, finely chopped
- ❖ 1 cup spinach leaves, washed and dried
- ❖ 1/2 cup grated mozzarella cheese (part-skim)

Step-by-Step Preparation:

- ✓ Lay out the whole wheat tortillas on a flat surface.
- ✓ Evenly spread the basil pesto over each tortilla.
- ✓ Sprinkle the finely chopped sun-dried tomatoes over the Pesto.
- ✓ Lay the spinach leaves over the tomatoes, creating an even layer.
- ✓ Sprinkle the grated mozzarella cheese atop the spinach.
- ✓ Carefully roll up each tortilla, ensuring it's tight but not torn.
- ✓ Using a sharp knife, slice the rolled tortillas into 1-inch pinwheels.
- ✓ Arrange on a platter and serve.

Nutritional Facts: (Per serving)

- ❖ Calories: 140
- ❖ Fat: 7g
- ❖ Protein: 5g
- ❖ Carbohydrates: 14g
- ❖ Fiber: 2g
- ❖ Sugars: 2g
- ❖ Sodium: 250mg

The Pesto and sun-dried Tomato Pinwheels are a dance of Mediterranean flavors wrapped in a heart-friendly package. As we delve deeper into low-cholesterol party plates in this chapter, these pinwheels emerge as a crowning jewel, elegantly intertwining taste and health. They capture the essence of a party—a burst of flavors, textures, and colors, all harmoniously coming together. Perfect for any gathering, they are a reminder that festive foods can seamlessly weave into heart-healthy narratives. With each bite, guests are transported to sun-soaked terrains and reassured of a culinary ethos that values both celebration and well-being.

Recipe 98: Seared Tuna Bites with Wasabi Dip

Embrace a gustatory journey to the East with the Seared Tuna Bites with Wasabi Dip. These bite-sized morsels offer the umami-richness of perfectly seared tuna, enhanced by the bold kick of wasabi. A sublime mix of taste and texture, these bites are an elegant fusion of simplicity and gourmet flavors, making them an undeniable hit for any festivity. As we journey through Party Plates: Celebrate the Low-Cholesterol Way, these tuna delights underscore that luxurious flavors can harmoniously coexist with heart-healthy choices.

Servings: 6

Prepping Time: 20 minutes

Cook Time: 8 minutes

Difficulty: Moderate

Ingredients:

- 1 lb fresh tuna steak
- 2 tbsp sesame oil
- Salt and pepper to taste

- ❖ 1/4 cup low-fat mayonnaise
- ❖ 1-2 tsp wasabi paste (adjust to taste)
- ❖ 1 tsp soy sauce
- ❖ 1 tbsp chopped green onions for garnish
- ❖ Sesame seeds for garnish

Step-by-Step Preparation:

- ✓ Heat sesame oil in a skillet over high heat.
- ✓ Season tuna steak with salt and pepper on both sides.
- ✓ Once the skillet is hot, sear the tuna steak on each side for 2-3 minutes, ensuring the center remains pink.
- ✓ Remove from heat and let it rest for a few minutes.
- ✓ Mix mayonnaise, wasabi paste, and soy sauce in a separate bowl to create the wasabi dip.
- ✓ Slice the seared tuna into bite-sized pieces.
- ✓ Arrange on a platter, garnishing with chopped green onions and sesame seeds.
- ✓ Serve with the wasabi dip on the side.

Nutritional Facts: (Per serving)

- ❖ Calories: 150
- ❖ Fat: 8g
- ❖ Protein: 17g
- ❖ Carbohydrates: 2g
- ❖ Fiber: 0g
- ❖ Sugars: 1g
- ❖ Sodium: 220mg

The Seared Tuna Bites with Wasabi Dip transport guests to culinary luxury while remaining steadfast in the ethos of heart health. These bites stand out as we explore low-cholesterol party plates in this chapter, exemplifying those exquisite flavors needn't be sacrificed in the name of health. Perfect for cocktail parties, soirées, or any celebratory gathering, they serve as a testament to the art of mind indulgence. Every bite is a perfect harmony of taste, texture, and health, reminding us that celebrations can always be a blend of gourmet experiences and well-being.

Recipe 99: Lemon & Herb Stuffed Mushrooms

Elevate the flavors of your party spread with Lemon and herb Stuffed Mushrooms, where rustic meets refinement. These bite-sized delights are filled with zesty and aromatic herb stuffing that complements the earthy notes of the mushrooms to perfection. They are a feast for the eyes and brimming with nutrients that align with heart-healthy guidelines. As we curate the exquisite lineup of Party Plates: Celebrate the Low-Cholesterol Way, these stuffed mushrooms are a dazzling example of how classic appetizers can be reinvented to be mouth-watering and health-conscious.

Servings: 8

Prepping Time: 20 minutes

Cook Time: 25 minutes

Difficulty: Moderate

Ingredients:

- 16 large mushroom caps, stems removed
- 1 cup breadcrumbs (preferably whole grain)

- 1/4 cup chopped fresh herbs (parsley, thyme, and chives)
- Zest of 1 lemon
- 1/4 cup grated Parmesan cheese
- 2 garlic cloves, minced
- 3 tbsp olive oil
- Salt and pepper to taste

Step-by-Step Preparation:

- Preheat the oven to 375°F (190°C).
- Combine breadcrumbs, herbs, lemon zest, Parmesan, garlic, and 2 tablespoons of olive oil in a mixing bowl. Season with salt and pepper and mix well.
- Brush mushroom caps with the remaining olive oil.
- Carefully stuff each mushroom cap with the breadcrumb mixture, pressing gently to ensure the filling is secure.
- Arrange the stuffed mushrooms on a baking sheet.
- Bake in the oven for 20-25 minutes or until the mushrooms are tender and the topping is golden brown.
- Allow them to cool slightly before serving.

Nutritional Facts: (Per serving)

- Calories: 110
- Fat: 6g
- Protein: 4g
- Carbohydrates: 10g
- Fiber: 2g
- Sugars: 1g
- Sodium: 130mg

Lemon and herb Stuffed Mushrooms bring together the comforting essence of baked appetizers and the vibrant allure of fresh herbs, creating an unforgettable taste experience. As we journey through our collection of low-cholesterol party plates, these mushrooms emerge as symbolic of the balance between gourmet pleasure and health. Ideal for festive gatherings, cocktail parties, or cozy evenings with loved ones, they encapsulate the joy of sharing food that's not just delectable but also heart-healthy. Each bite tells a tale of thoughtful culinary artistry, serving as a beautiful reminder that food, when made with love and care, is the heart and soul of any celebration.

Recipe 100: Dark Chocolate Dipped Strawberries

Indulge in the luscious union of sweet and bitter with Dark Chocolate Dipped Strawberries. These tempting treats beautifully merge the natural sweetness of ripe strawberries with the decadent allure of dark chocolate, creating a delightful and heart-healthy duet. As we unravel the wonders of Party Plates: Celebrate the Low-Cholesterol Way, these chocolaty gems exemplify that a touch of indulgence can coexist with health-conscious choices, making them the ultimate party favorite.

Servings: 8

Prepping Time: 15 minutes

Cook Time: 5 minutes

Difficulty: Easy

Ingredients:

- 16 ripe strawberries, washed and dried
- 6 oz high-quality dark chocolate (70% cocoa or higher)

- ❖ 1 tsp coconut oil (optional, for smoother consistency)
- ❖ Crushed nuts or desiccated coconut (optional for garnish)

Step-by-Step Preparation:

- ✓ Line a tray or plate with parchment paper.
- ✓ In a heat-proof bowl, melt the dark chocolate and coconut oil over a pot of simmering water, ensuring the water doesn't touch the bowl.
- ✓ Once melted, stir the chocolate mixture until smooth.
- ✓ Holding each strawberry by the stem, dip it into the melted chocolate, ensuring it's coated well.
- ✓ Allow excess chocolate to drip off before placing the strawberry on the parchment paper.
- ✓ If desired, sprinkle with crushed nuts or desiccated coconut while the chocolate is wet.
- ✓ Once all strawberries are coated, refrigerate for about 30 minutes or until the chocolate hardens.
- ✓ Serve chilled.

Nutritional Facts: (Per serving)

- ❖ Calories: 90
- ❖ Fat: 5g
- ❖ Protein: 1g
- ❖ Carbohydrates: 10g
- ❖ Fiber: 2g
- ❖ Sugars: 7g
- ❖ Sodium: 5mg

Dark Chocolate Dipped Strawberries are a celebration in every bite, blending the natural goodness of fruit with the indulgent richness of chocolate. As we showcase a symphony of low-cholesterol party treats in this chapter, these chocolate-coated jewels stand out, reminding us that celebrations can be both sweet and sensible. Whether it's a romantic evening, a festive gathering, or a moment of personal indulgence, these strawberries ensure that each bite is a heartwarming blend of taste and health. They beautifully encapsulate the joy of savoring life's little pleasures while staying committed to a heart-healthy journey.

Conclusion

Have you been searching for a comprehensive guide that seamlessly blends the promise of health with the joy of flavorful dishes? Look no further! **"Try The Best 100 Low Cholesterol Recipes"** curated by Divvey Wazsoya, is a culinary masterpiece that addresses the heart's needs without compromising the soul's cravings.

Each page of this book unveils a delicious secret, teaching you how to navigate the kitchen to produce delectable and heart-healthy dishes. With a harmonious blend of traditional and innovative recipes, Wazsoya takes you on a journey where every meal becomes a celebration. The vibrant photos accompanying each recipe don't just appeal to your eyes but also guide you in recreating these dishes to perfection.

Imagine hosting dinners where guests leave with satiated palates and the reassurance of a nutritious meal. Whether you're a novice in the kitchen or a seasoned chef, this cookbook offers fresh ideas, simplifying the art of low-cholesterol cooking.

Don't just dream of a healthier lifestyle; make it a reality! Dive into the culinary wonders of **"Try the Best 100 Low Cholesterol Recipes."** Trust in Divvey Wazsoya's expertise and let your kitchen be the birthplace of dishes that resonate with love, care, and health. Order your copy now and embark on a gastronomic journey that promises taste, health, and happiness. Embrace the art of cooking, where every dish is a heart-healthy masterpiece.

Printed in Great Britain
by Amazon